Civil War
Poetry and Prose

WALT WHITMAN

DOVER PUBLICATIONS, INC.
New York

DOVER THRIFT EDITIONS

GENERAL EDITOR: STANLEY APPELBAUM
EDITOR OF THIS VOLUME: CANDACE WARD

Bibliographical Note

This new collection, first published by Dover Publications, Inc., in 1995, contains poems reprinted from standard editions of *Leaves of Grass*. The prose selections are taken from standard texts of *Memoranda during the War* and Whitman's letters. (See the new Note, facing, for further bibliographical data.) The Note, explanatory footnotes and the alphabetical lists of the poems' titles and first lines have been specially prepared for this edition.

Library of Congress Cataloging-in-Publication Data

Whitman, Walt, 1819–1892.
    Civil War poetry and prose / Walt Whitman.
        p.   cm. — (Dover thrift editions)
    Includes index.
    ISBN 0-486-28507-3 (pbk.)
    1. United States—History—Civil War, 1861–1865—Poetry. 2. United States—History—Civil War, 1861–1865—Personal narratives. 3. Poets, American—19th century—Correspondence. 4. Whitman, Walt, 1819–1892—Correspondence. 5. War poetry, American. I. Title. II. Series.
PS3240   1996
811'.3—dc20
                                            95-607
                                           CIP

Manufactured in the United States of America
Dover Publications, Inc., 31 East 2nd Street, Mineola, N.Y. 11501

Note

WALT WHITMAN (1819–1892) was nearly 42 years old when the Civil War began. At that time, he was living in Brooklyn, New York, with his mother, contributing to the Brooklyn weekly *Standard* and trying to find a publisher for *Leaves of Grass*, which had been through three editions since its first publication in 1855. His brother George, ten years younger, immediately enlisted in the 51st New York Volunteers; Whitman's patriotism—no less fervent than his brother's—exhibited itself in his writings. In the excitement and indignation following the opening battle of Fort Sumter, he began composing a volume of war poems, *Drum-Taps*, most of which he finished before the end of 1862.

In December 1862, Whitman and his family received notice that George had been wounded at the first battle of Fredericksburg, Virginia. Whitman immediately traveled south to find him, first stopping in Washington. There Whitman searched the makeshift army hospitals that were being set up in churches, private mansions and government offices to accommodate the overwhelming influx of wounded soldiers. Though Whitman did not find his brother, he saw for the first time the true costs of the War. After two days, he left Washington for the front in Virginia where he found George, whose wound had not been serious. Here, too, Whitman was surrounded by the wounded and the dying.

When Whitman returned to Washington nine days later, he wrote to his mother that he would remain there "to see if I can get any employment at anything." Whitman stayed in Washington throughout most of the War, working as a government clerk and writing articles and essays for the New York newspapers. But Whitman considered his real work tending the sick and wounded soldiers—Union and Confederate—that came through the Washington hospitals. He became a familiar sight on the wards, making his rounds, comforting soldiers, writing letters for them, reading to them or simply sitting by their sides. His own impressions he recorded in small notebooks he carried with him, and which were later published as *Memoranda during the War* (1875–76). As these journal entries show, Whitman was profoundly moved by his hospital experiences. Reading his memoranda in light of the patriotic fervor of the early war poems, such as "Beat! Beat! Drums!" or "Bathed in War's

Perfume," one can see the transition in Whitman's responses as he encountered the realities of the War.

The compassion and sorrow Whitman felt are especially evident in his descriptions of President Lincoln, to whom he was particularly drawn. Living and working in such close proximity to the White House and Capitol, Whitman often saw the President. Whitman—a staunch Unionist himself—came to view Lincoln as a living symbol of the country toin apart. After seeing him on the evening following his second inauguration, Whitman wrote: "He . . . look'd very much worn and tired; the lines, indeed, of vast responsibilities, intricate questions, and demands of life and death, cut deeper than ever upon his dark brown face; yet all the old goodness, tenderness, sadness, and canny shrewdness, underneath the furrows. (I never see that man without feeling that he is one to become personally attach'd to . . .)." The grief Whitman felt on Lincoln's assassination was as deep as any he had experienced during the war, and his elegy "When Lilacs Last in the Dooryard Bloom'd" is perhaps the most moving poem in American literature.

The poems in this volume (except "Bathed in War's Perfume" and "Solid, Ironical, Rolling Orb") are reprinted from a standard text of the 1891–92 "Deathbed Edition" of *Leaves of Grass*. Most appeared earlier, in either the 1865 volume *Drum-Taps* or *Sequel to Drum-Taps* (also published in 1865), and were incorporated into later editions of *Leaves of Grass*. ("Bathed in War's Perfume" and "Solid, Ironical, Rolling Orb" were first published in *Drum-Taps* and appeared in subsequent editions of *Leaves of Grass* until the 1881 edition, from which they were dropped.) There are two dates following each poem; on the left is the year the poem was composed (if known) or first published, and on the right is the year of its final revision and inclusion in *Leaves of Grass*.

Contents

NOTE: Those poems followed by (*DT*) first appeared in the volume *Drum-Taps* (1865); those followed by (*SDT*) first appeared in *Sequel to Drum-Taps* (1865–66).

POEMS FROM *LEAVES OF GRASS* (1891–92)

First O Songs for a Prelude

First O songs for a prelude,
Lightly strike on the stretch'd tympanum pride and joy in my city,
How she led the rest to arms, how she gave the cue,
How at once with lithe limbs unwaiting a moment she sprang,
(O superb! O Manhattan, my own, my peerless!
O strongest you in the hour of danger, in crisis! O truer than steel!)
How you sprang — how you threw off the costumes of peace with indif-
    ferent hand,
How your soft opera-music changed, and the drum and fife were heard
    in their stead,
How you led to the war, (that shall serve for our prelude, songs of
    soldiers,)
How Manhattan drum-taps led.

Forty years had I in my city seen soldiers parading,
Forty years as a pageant, till unawares the lady of this teeming and
    turbulent city,
Sleepless amid her ships, her houses, her incalculable wealth,
With her million children around her, suddenly,
At dead of night, at news from the south,
Incens'd struck with clinch'd hand the pavement.

A shock electric, the night sustain'd it,
Till with ominous hum our hive at daybreak pour'd out its myriads.

From the houses then and the workshops, and through all the doorways,
Leapt they tumultuous, and lo! Manhattan arming.

To the drum-taps prompt,
The young men falling in and arming,
The mechanics arming, (the trowel, the jack-plane, the blacksmith's
    hammer, tost aside with precipitation,)
The lawyer leaving his office and arming, the judge leaving the court,

The driver deserting his wagon in the street, jumping down, throwing
the reins abruptly down on the horses' backs,
The salesman leaving the store, the boss, book-keeper, porter, all leav-
ing;
Squads gather everywhere by common consent and arm,
The new recruits, even boys, the old men show them how to wear their
accoutrements, they buckle the straps carefully,
Outdoors, arming, indoors arming, the flash of the musket-barrels,
The white tents cluster in camps, the arm'd sentries around, the sunrise
cannon and again at sunset,
Arm'd regiments arrive every day, pass through the city, and embark
from the wharves,
(How good they look as they tramp down to the river, sweaty, with their
guns on their shoulders!
How I love them! how I could hug them, with their brown faces and
their clothes and knapsacks cover'd with dust!)
The blood of the city up — arm'd! arm'd! the cry everywhere,
The flags flung out from the steeples of churches and from all the public
buildings and stores,
The tearful parting, the mother kisses her son, the son kisses his mother,
(Loth is the mother to part, yet not a word does she speak to detain him,)
The tumultuous escort, the ranks of policemen preceding, clearing the
way,
The unpent enthusiasm, the wild cheers of the crowd for their favorites,
The artillery, the silent cannons bright as gold, drawn along, rumble
lightly over the stones,
(Silent cannons, soon to cease your silence,
Soon unlimber'd to begin the red business;)
All the mutter of preparation, all the determin'd arming,
The hospital service, the lint, bandages and medicines,
The women volunteering for nurses, the work begun for in earnest, no
mere parade now;
War! an arm'd race is advancing! the welcome for battle, no turning
away;
War! be it weeks, months, or years, an arm'd race is advancing to
welcome it.

Mannahatta a-march — and it's O to sing it well!
It's O for a manly life in the camp.

And the sturdy artillery,
The guns bright as gold, the work for giants, to serve well the guns,

Unlimber them! (no more as the past forty years for salute or courtesies
    merely,
Put in something now besides powder and wadding.)

And you lady of ships, you Mannahatta,
Old matron of this proud, friendly, turbulent city,
Often in peace and wealth you were pensive or covertly frown'd amid all
    your children,
But now you smile with joy exulting old Mannahatta.

1865   1867

Eighteen Sixty-One

Arm'd year — year of the struggle,
No dainty rhymes or sentimental love verses for you terrible year,
Not you as some pale poetling seated at a desk lisping cadenzas piano,
But as a strong man erect, clothed in blue clothes, advancing, carrying a
    rifle on your shoulder,
With well-gristled body and sunburnt face and hands, with a knife in the
    belt at your side,
As I heard you shouting loud, your sonorous voice ringing across the
    continent,
Your masculine voice O year, as rising amid the great cities,
Amid the men of Manhattan I saw you as one of the workmen, the
    dwellers in Manhattan,
Or with large steps crossing the prairies out of Illinois and Indiana,
Rapidly crossing the West with springy gait and descending the Alle-
    ghanies,
Or down from the great lakes or in Pennsylvania, or on deck along the
    Ohio river,
Or southward along the Tennessee or Cumberland rivers, or at Chat-
    tanooga on the mountain top,
Saw I your gait and saw I your sinewy limbs clothed in blue, bearing
    weapons, robust year,
Heard your determin'd voice launch'd forth again and again,
Year that suddenly sang by the mouths of the round-lipp'd cannon,
I repeat you, hurrying, crashing, sad, distracted year.

(1861?)   1867

Beat! Beat! Drums!

Beat! beat! drums! — blow! bugles! blow!
Through the windows — through doors — burst like a ruthless force,
Into the solemn church, and scatter the congregation,
Into the school where the scholar is studying;
Leave not the bridegroom quiet — no happiness must he have now with
   his bride,
Nor the peaceful farmer any peace, ploughing his field or gathering his
   grain,
So fierce you whirr and pound you drums — so shrill you bugles blow.

Beat! beat! drums! — blow! bugles! blow!
Over the traffic of cities — over the rumble of wheels in the streets;
Are beds prepared for sleepers at night in the houses? no sleepers must
   sleep in those beds,
No bargainers' bargains by day — no brokers or speculators — would they
   continue?
Would the talkers be talking? would the singer attempt to sing?
Would the lawyer rise in the court to state his case before the judge?
Then rattle quicker, heavier drums — you bugles wilder blow.

Beat! beat! drums! — blow! bugles! blow!
Make no parley — stop for no expostulation,
Mind not the timid — mind not the weeper or prayer,
Mind not the old man beseeching the young man,
Let not the child's voice be heard, nor the mother's entreaties,
Make even the trestles to shake the dead where they lie awaiting the
   hearses,
So strong you thump O terrible drums — so loud you bugles blow.

1861   *1867*

From Paumanok Starting I Fly Like a Bird

From Paumanok starting I fly like a bird,
Around and around to soar to sing the idea of all,
To the north betaking myself to sing there arctic songs,

To Kanada till I absorb Kanada in myself, to Michigan then,
To Wisconsin, Iowa, Minnesota, to sing their songs, (they are inimitable;)
Then to Ohio and Indiana to sing theirs, to Missouri and Kansas and Arkansas to sing theirs,
To Tennessee and Kentucky, to the Carolinas and Georgia to sing theirs,
To Texas and so along up toward California, to roam accepted everywhere;
To sing first, (to the tap of the war-drum if need be,)
The idea of all, of the Western world one and inseparable,
And then the song of each member of these States.

1865   *1867*

Song of the Banner at Daybreak

Poet

O a new song, a free song,
Flapping, flapping, flapping, flapping, by sounds, by voices clearer,
By the wind's voice and that of the drum,
By the banner's voice and child's voice and sea's voice and father's voice,
Low on the ground and high in the air,
On the ground where father and child stand,
In the upward air where their eyes turn,
Where the banner at daybreak is flapping.

Words! book-words! what are you?
Words no more, for hearken and see,
My song is there in the open air, and I must sing,
With the banner and pennant a-flapping.

I'll weave the chord and twine in,
Man's desire and babe's desire, I'll twine them in, I'll put in life,
I'll put the bayonet's flashing point, I'll let bullets and slugs whizz,
(As one carrying a symbol and menace far into the future,
Crying with trumpet voice, *Arouse and beware! Beware and arouse!*)
I'll pour the verse with streams of blood, full of volition, full of joy,
Then loosen, launch forth, to go and compete,
With the banner and pennant a-flapping.

Pennant

Come up here, bard, bard,
Come up here, soul, soul,
Come up here, dear little child,
To fly in the clouds and winds with me, and play with the measureless
      light.

Child

Father what is that in the sky beckoning to me with long finger?
And what does it say to me all the while?

Father

Nothing my babe you see in the sky,
And nothing at all to you it says — but look you my babe,
Look at these dazzling things in the houses, and see you the money-
      shops opening,
And see you the vehicles preparing to crawl along the streets with goods;
These, ah these, how valued and toil'd for these!
How envied by all the earth!

Poet

Fresh and rosy red the sun is mounting high,
On floats the sea in distant blue careering through its channels,
On floats the wind over the breast of the sea setting in toward land,
The great steady wind from west or west-by-south,
Floating so buoyant with milk-white foam on the waters.

But I am not the sea nor the red sun,
I am not the wind with girlish laughter,
Not the immense wind which strengthens, not the wind which lashes,
Not the spirit that ever lashes its own body to terror and death,
But I am that which unseen comes and sings, sings, sings,
Which babbles in brooks and scoots in showers on the land,
Which the birds know in the woods mornings and evenings,
And the shore-sands know and the hissing wave, and that banner and
      pennant,
Aloft there flapping and flapping.

Child

O father it is alive — it is full of people — it has children,
O now it seems to me it is talking to its children,

I hear it — it talks to me — O it is wonderful!
O it stretches — it spreads and runs so fast — O my father,
It is so broad it covers the whole sky.

Father

Cease, cease, my foolish babe,
What you are saying is sorrowful to me, much it displeases me;
Behold with the rest again I say, behold not banners and pennants aloft,
But the well-prepared pavements behold, and mark the solid-wall'd
  houses.

Banner and Pennant

Speak to the child O bard out of Manhattan,
To our children all, or north or south of Manhattan,
Point this day, leaving all the rest, to us over all — and yet we know not
  why,
For what are we, mere strips of cloth profiting nothing,
Only flapping in the wind?

Poet

I hear and see not strips of cloth alone,
I hear the tramp of armies, I hear the challenging sentry,
I hear the jubilant shouts of millions of men, I hear Liberty!
I hear the drums beat and the trumpets blowing,
I myself move abroad swift-rising flying then,
I use the wings of the land-bird and use the wings of the sea-bird, and
  look down as from a height,
I do not deny the precious results of peace, I see populous cities with
  wealth incalculable,
I see numberless farms, I see the farmers working in their fields or barns,
I see mechanics working, I see buildings everywhere founded, going up,
  or finish'd,
I see trains of cars swiftly speeding along railroad tracks drawn by the
  locomotives,
I see the stores, depots, of Boston, Baltimore, Charleston, New Orleans,
I see far in the West the immense area of grain, I dwell awhile hovering,
I pass to the lumber forests of the North, and again to the Southern
  plantation, and again to California;
Sweeping the whole I see the countless profit, the busy gatherings,
  earn'd wages,
See the Identity formed out of thirty-eight spacious and haughty States,
  (and many more to come,)

See forts on the shores of harbors, see ships sailing in and out;
Then over all, (aye! aye!) my little and lengthen'd pennant shaped like a
     sword,
Runs swiftly up indicating war and defiance — and now the halyards
     have rais'd it,
Side of my banner broad and blue, side of my starry banner,
Discarding peace over all the sea and land.

Banner and Pennant

Yet louder, higher, stronger, bard! yet farther, wider cleave!
No longer let our children deem us riches and peace alone,
We may be terror and carnage, and are so now,
Not now are we any one of these spacious and haughty States, (nor any
     five, nor ten,)
Nor market nor depot we, nor money-bank in the city,
But these and all, and the brown and spreading land, and the mines
     below, are ours,
And the shores of the sea are ours, and the rivers great and small,
And the fields they moisten, and the crops and the fruits are ours,
Bays and channels and ships sailing in and out are ours — while we over
     all,
Over the area spread below, the three or four millions of square miles,
     the capitals,
The forty millions of people, — O bard! in life and death supreme,
We, even we, henceforth flaunt out masterful, high up above,
Not for the present alone, for a thousand years chanting through you,
This song to the soul of one poor little child.

Child

O my father I like not the houses,
They will never to me be anything, nor do I like money,
But to mount up there I would like, O father dear, that banner I like,
That pennant I would be and must be.

Father

Child of mine you fill me with anguish,
To be that pennant would be too fearful,
Little you know what it is this day, and after this day, forever,
It is to gain nothing, but risk and defy everything,
Forward to stand in front of wars — and O, such wars! — what have you to
     do with them?
With passions of demons, slaughter, premature death?

Banner

Demons and death then I sing,
Put in all, aye all will I, sword-shaped pennant for war,
And a pleasure new and ecstatic, and the prattled yearning of children,
Blent with the sounds of the peaceful land and the liquid wash of the
    sea,
And the black ships fighting on the sea envelop'd in smoke,
And the icy cool of the far, far north, with rustling cedars and pines,
And the whirr of drums and the sound of soldiers marching, and the hot
    sun shining south,
And the beach-waves combing over the beach on my Eastern shore, and
    my Western shore the same,
And all between those shores, and my ever running Mississippi with
    bends and chutes,
And my Illinois fields, and my Kansas fields, and my fields of Missouri,
The Continent, devoting the whole identity without reserving an atom,
Pour in! whelm that which asks, which sings, with all and the yield of all,
Fusing and holding, claiming, devouring the whole,
No more with tender lip, nor musical labial sound,
But out of the night emerging for good, our voice persuasive no more,
Croaking like crows here in the wind.

Poet

My limbs, my veins dilate, my theme is clear at last,
Banner so broad advancing out of the night, I sing you haughty and
    resolute,
I burst through where I waited long, too long, deafen'd and blinded,
My hearing and tongue are come to me, (a little child taught me,)
I hear from above O pennant of war your ironical call and demand,
Insensate! insensate (yet I at any rate chant you,) O banner!
Not houses of peace indeed are you, nor any nor all their prosperity, (if
    need be, you shall again have every one of those houses to destroy
    them,
You thought not to destroy those valuable houses, standing fast, full of
    comfort, built with money,
May they stand fast, then? not an hour except you above them and all
    stand fast;)
O banner, not money so precious are you, not farm produce you, nor the
    material good nutriment,
Nor excellent stores, nor landed on wharves from the ships,
Not the superb ships with sail-power or steam-power, fetching and
    carrying cargoes,

Nor machinery, vehicles, trade, nor revenues — but you as henceforth I
   see you,
Running up out of the night, bringing your cluster of stars, (ever-
   enlarging stars,)
Divider of daybreak you, cutting the air, touch'd by the sun, measuring
   the sky,
(Passionately seen and yearn'd for by one poor little child,
While others remain busy or smartly talking, forever teaching thrift,
   thrift;)
O you up there! O pennant! where you undulate like a snake hissing so
   curious,
Out of reach, an idea only, yet furiously fought for, risking bloody death,
   loved by me,
So loved — O you banner leading the day with stars brought from the
   night!
Valueless, object of eyes, over all and demanding all — (absolute owner
   of all) — O banner and pennant!
I too leave the rest — great as it is, it is nothing — houses, machines are
   nothing — I see them not,
I see but you, O warlike pennant! O banner so broad, with stripes, I sing
   you only,
Flapping up there in the wind.

(1861–2?)   *1881*

Virginia — The West

The noble sire fallen on evil days,
I saw with hand uplifted, menacing, brandishing,
(Memories of old in abeyance, love and faith in abeyance,)
The insane knife toward the Mother of All.

The noble son on sinewy feet advancing,
I saw, out of the land of prairies, land of Ohio's waters and of Indiana,
To the rescue the stalwart giant hurry his plenteous offspring,
Drest in blue, bearing their trusty rifles on their shoulders.

Then the Mother of All with calm voice speaking,
As to you Rebellious, (I seemed to hear her say,) why strive against me,
    and why seek my life?
When you yourself forever provide to defend me?
For you provided me Washington — and now these also.

1872   1881

Cavalry Crossing a Ford

A line in long array where they wind betwixt green islands,
They take a serpentine course, their arms flash in the sun — hark to the
    musical clank,
Behold the silvery river, in it the splashing horses loitering stop to drink,
Behold the brown-faced men, each group, each person a picture, the
    negligent rest on the saddles,
Some emerge on the opposite bank, others are just entering the ford —
    while,
Scarlet and blue and snowy white,
The guidon flags flutter gayly in the wind.

1865   1871

Bivouac on a Mountain Side

I see before me now a traveling army halting,
Below a fertile valley spread, with barns and the orchards of summer,
Behind, the terraced sides of a mountain, abrupt, in places rising high,
Broken, with rocks, with clinging cedars, with tall shapes dingily seen,
The numerous camp-fires scatter'd near and far, some away up on the
    mountain,
The shadowy forms of men and horses, looming, large-sized, flickering,
And over all the sky — the sky! far, far out of reach, studded, breaking
    out, the eternal stars.

1865   1871

An Army Corps on the March*

With its cloud of skirmishers in advance,
With now the sound of a single shot snapping like a whip, and now an
    irregular volley,
The swarming ranks press on and on, the dense brigades press on,
Glittering dimly, toiling under the sun—the dust-cover'd men,
In columns rise and fall to the undulations of the ground,
With artillery interspers'd—the wheels rumble, the horses sweat,
As the army corps advances.

1865–6   *1871*

By the Bivouac's Fitful Flame

By the bivouac's fitful flame,
A procession winding around me, solemn and sweet and slow—but first
    I note,
The tents of the sleeping army, the fields' and woods' dim outline,
The darkness lit by spots of kindled fire, the silence,
Like a phantom far or near an occasional figure moving,
The shrubs and trees, (as I lift my eyes they seem to be stealthily
    watching me,)
While wind in procession thoughts, O tender and wondrous thoughts,
Of life and death, of home and the past and loved, and of those that are
    far away;
A solemn and slow procession there as I sit on the ground,
By the bivouac's fitful flame.

1865   *1867*

Come Up from the Fields Father

Come up from the fields father, here's a letter from our Pete,
And come to the front door mother, here's a letter from thy dear son.

Lo, 'tis autumn,
Lo, where the trees, deeper green, yellower and redder,

---

* Entitled "An Army on the March" in *Sequel to Drum-Taps*.

Cool and sweeten Ohio's villages with leaves fluttering in the moderate
    wind,
Where apples ripe in the orchards hang and grapes on the trellis'd vines,
(Smell you the smell of the grapes on the vines?
Smell you the buckwheat where the bees were lately buzzing?)

Above all, lo, the sky so calm, so transparent after the rain, and with
    wondrous clouds,
Below too, all calm, all vital and beautiful, and the farm prospers well.

Down in the fields all prospers well,
But now from the fields come father, come at the daughter's call,
And come to the entry mother, to the front door come right away.

Fast as she can she hurries, something ominous, her steps trembling,
She does not tarry to smooth her hair nor adjust her cap.

Open the envelope quickly,
O this is not our son's writing, yet his name is sign'd,
O a strange hand writes for our dear son, O stricken mother's soul!
All swims before her eyes, flashes with black, she catches the main words
    only,
Sentences broken, *gunshot wound in the breast, cavalry skirmish, taken
    to hospital,*
At present low, but will soon be better.

Ah now the single figure to me,
Amid all teeming and wealthy Ohio with all its cities and farms,
Sickly white in the face and dull in the head, very faint,
By the jamb of a door leans.

Grieve not so, dear mother, (the just-grown daughter speaks through her
    sobs,
The little sisters huddle around speechless and dismay'd,)
See, dearest mother, the letter says Pete will soon be better.

Alas poor boy, he will never be better, (nor may-be needs to be better,
    that brave and simple soul,)
While they stand at home at the door he is dead already,
The only son is dead.

But the mother needs to be better,
She with thin form presently drest in black,

By day her meals untouch'd, then at night fitfully sleeping, often wak-
    ing,
In the midnight waking, weeping, longing with one deep longing,
O that she might withdraw unnoticed, silent from life escape and
    withdraw,
To follow, to seek, to be with her dear dead son.

1865   1867

Vigil Strange I Kept on the Field One Night

Vigil strange I kept on the field one night;
When you my son and my comrade dropt at my side that day,
One look I but gave which your dear eyes return'd with a look I shall
    never forget,
One touch of your hand to mine O boy, reach'd up as you lay on the
    ground,
Then onward I sped in the battle, the even-contested battle,
Till late in the night reliev'd to the place at last again I made my way,
Found you in death so cold dear comrade, found your body son of
    responding kisses, (never again on earth responding,)
Bared your face in the starlight, curious the scene, cool blew the
    moderate night-wind,
Long there and then in vigil I stood, dimly around me the battlefield
    spreading,
Vigil wondrous and vigil sweet there in the fragrant silent night,
But not a tear fell, not even a long-drawn sigh, long, long I gazed,
Then on the earth partially reclining sat by your side leaning my chin in
    my hands,
Passing sweet hours, immortal and mystic hours with you dearest
    comrade — not a tear, not a word,
Vigil of silence, love and death, vigil for you my son and my soldier,
As onward silently stars aloft, eastward new ones upward stole,
Vigil final for you brave boy, (I could not save you, swift was your death,
I faithfully loved you and cared for you living, I think we shall surely
    meet again,)
Till at latest lingering of the night, indeed just as the dawn appear'd,
My comrade I wrapt in his blanket, envelop'd well his form,
Folded the blanket well, tucking it carefully over head and carefully
    under feet,

And there and then and bathed by the rising sun, my son in his grave, in
    his rude-dug grave I deposited,
Ending my vigil strange with that, vigil of night and battlefield dim,
Vigil for boy of responding kisses, (never again on earth responding,)
Vigil for comrade swiftly slain, vigil I never forget, how as day brighten'd,
I rose from the chill ground and folded my soldier well in his blanket,
And buried him where he fell.

1865   *1867*

A March in the Ranks Hard-Prest, and the Road Unknown

A march in the ranks hard-prest, and the road unknown,
A route through a heavy wood with muffled steps in the darkness,
Our army foil'd with loss severe, and the sullen remnant retreating,
Till after midnight glimmer upon us the lights of a dim-lighted building,
We come to an open space in the woods, and halt by the dim-lighted
    building,
'Tis a large old church at the crossing roads, now an impromptu hos-
    pital,
Entering but for a minute I see a sight beyond all the pictures and poems
    ever made,
Shadows of deepest, deepest black, just lit by moving candles and lamps,
And by one great pitchy torch stationary with wild red flame and clouds
    of smoke,
By these, crowds, groups of forms vaguely I see on the floor, some in the
    pews laid down,
At my feet more distinctly a soldier, a mere lad, in danger of bleeding to
    death, (he is shot in the abdomen,)
I stanch the blood temporarily, (the youngster's face is white as a lily,)
Then before I depart I sweep my eyes o'er the scene fain to absorb it all,
Faces, varieties, postures beyond description, most in obscurity, some of
    them dead,
Surgeons operating, attendants holding lights, the smell of ether, the
    odor of blood,
The crowd, O the crowd of the bloody forms, the yard outside also fill'd,
Some on the bare ground, some on planks or stretchers, some in the
    death-spasm sweating,
An occasional scream or cry, the doctor's shouted orders or calls,

The glisten of the little steel instruments catching the glint of the
    torches,
These I resume as I chant, I see again the forms, I smell the odor,
Then hear outside the orders given, *Fall in, my men, fall in;*
But first I bend to the dying lad, his eyes open, a half-smile gives he me,
Then the eyes close, calmly close, and I speed forth to the darkness,
Resuming, marching, ever in darkness marching, on in the ranks,
The unknown road still marching.

1865   *1867*

A Sight in Camp in the Daybreak Gray and Dim

A sight in camp in the daybreak gray and dim,
As from my tent I emerge so early sleepless,
As slow I walk in the cool fresh air the path near by the hospital tent,
Three forms I see on stretchers lying, brought out there untended lying,
Over each the blanket spread, ample brownish woolen blanket,
Gray and heavy blanket, folding, covering all.

Curious I halt and silent stand,
Then with light fingers I from the face of the nearest the first just lift the
    blanket;
Who are you elderly man so gaunt and grim, with well-gray'd hair, and
    flesh all sunken about the eyes?
Who are you my dear comrade?

Then to the second I step — and who are you my child and darling?
Who are you sweet boy with cheeks yet blooming?

Then to the third — a face nor child nor old, very calm, as of beautiful
    yellow-white ivory;
Young man I think I know you — I think this face is the face of the Christ
    himself,
Dead and divine and brother of all, and here again he lies.

1865   *1867*

As Toilsome I Wander'd Virginia's Woods

As toilsome I wander'd Virginia's woods,
To the music of rustling leaves kick'd by my feet, (for 'twas autumn,)
I mark'd at the foot of a tree the grave of a soldier;
Mortally wounded he and buried on the retreat, (easily all could I
    understand,)
The halt of a mid-day hour, when up! no time to lose — yet this sign left,
On a tablet scrawl'd and nail'd on the tree by the grave,
Bold, cautious, true, and my loving comrade.

Long, long I muse, then on my way go wandering,
Many a changeful season to follow, and many a scene of life,
Yet at times through changeful season and scene, abrupt, alone, or in
    the crowded street,
Comes before me the unknown soldier's grave, comes the inscription
    rude in Virginia's woods,
Bold, cautious, true, and my loving comrade.

1865   1867

Year That Trembled and Reel'd Beneath Me

Year that trembled and reel'd beneath me!
Your summer wind was warm enough, yet the air I breathed froze me,
A thick gloom fell through the sunshine and darken'd me,
Must I change my triumphant songs? said I to myself,
Must I indeed learn to chant the cold dirges of the baffled?
And sullen hymns of defeat?

1865   1867

The Wound-Dresser*

1 An old man bending I come among new faces,
     Years looking backward resuming in answer to children,
     Come tell us old man, as from young men and maidens that love me,
     (Arous'd and angry, I'd thought to beat the alarum, and urge relentless
           war,
     But soon my fingers fail'd me, my face droop'd and I resign'd myself,
     To sit by the wounded and soothe them, or silently watch the dead;)
     Years hence of these scenes, of these furious passions, these chances,
     Of unsurpass'd heroes, (was one side so brave? the other was equally
           brave;)
     Now be witness again, paint the mightiest armies of earth,
     Of those armies so rapid so wondrous what saw you to tell us?
     What stays with you latest and deepest? of curious panics,
     Of hard-fought engagements or sieges tremendous what deepest re-
           mains?

2 O maidens and young men I love and that love me,
     What you ask of my days those the strangest and sudden your talking
           recalls,
     Soldier alert I arrive after a long march cover'd with sweat and dust,
     In the nick of time I come, plunge in the fight, loudly shout in the
           rush of successful charge,
     Enter the captur'd works — yet lo, like a swift running river they fade,
     Pass and are gone they fade — I dwell not on soldiers' perils or soldiers'
           joys,
     (Both I remember well — many of the hardships, few the joys, yet I
           was content.)

     But in silence, in dreams' projections,
     While the world of gain and appearance and mirth goes on,
     So soon what is over forgotten, and waves wash the imprints off the
           sand,
     With hinged knees returning I enter the doors, (while for you up
           there,
     Whoever you are, follow without noise and be of strong heart.)

---

* Entitled "The Dresser" in *Drum-Taps*.

Bearing the bandages, water and sponge,
Straight and swift to my wounded I go,
Where they lie on the ground after the battle brought in,
Where their priceless blood reddens the grass the ground,
Or to the rows of the hospital tent, or under the roof'd hospital,
To the long rows of cots up and down each side I return,
To each and all one after another I draw near, not one do I miss,
An attendant follows holding a tray, he carries a refuse pail,
Soon to be fill'd with clotted rags and blood, emptied, and fill'd again.

I onward go, I stop,
With hinged knees and steady hand to dress wounds,
I am firm with each, the pangs are sharp yet unavoidable,
One turns to me his appealing eyes — poor boy! I never knew you,
Yet I think I could not refuse this moment to die for you, if that would
     save you.

3 On, on I go, (open doors of time! open hospital doors!)
   The crush'd head I dress, (poor crazed hand tear not the bandage
        away,)
   The neck of the cavalry-man with the bullet through and through I
        examine,
   Hard the breathing rattles, quite glazed already the eye, yet life
        struggles hard,
   (Come sweet death! be persuaded O beautiful death!
   In mercy come quickly.)

   From the stump of the arm, the amputated hand,
   I undo the clotted lint, remove the slough, wash off the matter and
        blood,
   Back on his pillow the soldier bends with curv'd neck and side falling
        head,
   His eyes are closed, his face is pale, he dares not look on the bloody
        stump,
   And has not yet look'd on it.

   I dress a wound in the side, deep, deep,
   But a day or two more, for see the frame all wasted and sinking,
   And the yellow-blue countenance see.

   I dress the perforated shoulder, the foot with the bullet-wound,
   Cleanse the one with a gnawing and putrid gangrene, so sickening, so
        offensive,
   While the attendant stands behind aside me holding the tray and pail.

I am faithful, I do not give out,
The fractur'd thigh, the knee, the wound in the abdomen,
These and more I dress with impassive hand, (yet deep in my breast a
    fire, a burning flame.)

4 Thus in silence in dreams' projections,
Returning, resuming, I thread my way through the hospitals,
The hurt and wounded I pacify with soothing hand,
I sit by the restless all the dark night, some are so young,
Some suffer so much, I recall the experience sweet and sad,
(Many a soldier's loving arms about this neck have cross'd and rested,
Many a soldier's kiss dwells on these bearded lips.)

1865   1881

Long, Too Long America*

Long, too long America,
Traveling roads all even and peaceful you learn'd from joys and prosper-
    ity only,
But now, ah now, to learn from crises of anguish, advancing, grappling
    with direst fate and recoiling not,
And now to conceive and show to the world what your children en-
    masse really are,
(For who except myself has yet conceiv'd what your children en-masse
    really are?)

1865   1881

Dirge for Two Veterans

        The last sunbeam
Lightly falls from the finish'd Sabbath,
On the pavement here, and there beyond it is looking,
        Down a new-made double grave.

---

* Entitled "Long, Too Long, O Land" in *Drum-Taps*.

Lo, the moon ascending,
Up from the east the silvery round moon,
Beautiful over the house-tops, ghastly, phantom moon,
Immense and silent moon.

I see a sad procession,
And I hear the sound of coming full-key'd bugles,
All the channels of the city streets they're flooding,
As with voices and with tears.

I hear the great drums pounding,
And the small drums steady whirring,
And every blow of the great convulsive drums,
Strikes me through and through.

For the son is brought with the father,
(In the foremost ranks of the fierce assault they fell,
Two veterans son and father dropt together,
And the double grave awaits them.)

Now nearer blow the bugles,
And the drums strike more convulsive,
And the daylight o'er the pavement quite has faded,
And the strong dead-march enwraps me.

In the eastern sky up-buoying,
The sorrowful vast phantom moves illumin'd,
('Tis some mother's large transparent face,
In heaven brighter growing.)

O strong dead-march you please me!
O moon immense with your silvery face you soothe me!
O my soldiers twain! O my veterans passing to burial!
What I have I also give you.

The moon gives you light,
And the bugles and the drums give you music,
And my heart, O my soldiers, my veterans,
My heart gives you love.

1865–6   1881

Over the Carnage Rose Prophetic a Voice

Over the carnage rose prophetic a voice,
Be not dishearten'd, affection shall solve the problems of freedom yet,
Those who love each other shall become invincible,
They shall yet make Columbia victorious.

Sons of the Mother of All, you shall yet be victorious,
You shall yet laugh to scorn the attacks of all the remainder of the earth.

No danger shall balk Columbia's lovers,
If need be a thousand shall sternly immolate themselves for one.

One from Massachusetts shall be a Missourian's comrade,
From Maine and from hot Carolina, and another an Oregonese, shall
    be friends triune,
More precious to each other than all the riches of the earth.

To Michigan, Florida perfumes shall tenderly come,
Not the perfumes of flowers, but sweeter, and wafted beyond death.

It shall be customary in the houses and streets to see manly affection,
The most dauntless and rude shall touch face to face lightly,
The dependence of Liberty shall be lovers,
The continuance of Equality shall be comrades.

These shall tie you and band you stronger than hoops of iron,
I, ecstatic, O partners! O lands, with the love of lovers tie you.

(Were you looking to be held together by lawyers?
Or by an agreement on a paper? or by arms?
Nay, nor the world, nor any living thing, will so cohere.)

1860   *1867*

The Artilleryman's Vision*

While my wife at my side lies slumbering, and the wars are over long,
And my head on the pillow rests at home, and the vacant midnight
    passes,
And through the stillness, through the dark, I hear, just hear, the breath
    of my infant,
There in the room as I wake from sleep this vision presses upon me;
The engagement opens there and then in fantasy unreal,
The skirmishers begin, they crawl cautiously ahead, I hear the irregular
    snap! snap!
I hear the sounds of the different missiles, the short *t-h-t! t-h-t!* of the
    rifle-balls,
I see the shells exploding leaving small white clouds, I hear the great
    shells shrieking as they pass,
The grape like the hum and whirr of wind through the trees, (tumul-
    tuous now the contest rages,)
All the scenes at the batteries rise in detail before me again,
The crashing and smoking, the pride of the men in their pieces,
The chief-gunner ranges and sights his piece and selects a fuse of the
    right time,
After firing I see him lean aside and look eagerly off to note the effect;
Elsewhere I hear the cry of a regiment charging, (the young colonel
    leads himself this time with brandish'd sword,)
I see the gaps cut by the enemy's volleys, (quickly fill'd up, no delay,)
I breathe the suffocating smoke, then the flat clouds hover low conceal-
    ing all;
Now a strange lull for a few seconds, not a shot fired on either side,
Then resumed the chaos louder than ever, with eager calls and orders of
    officers,
While from some distant part of the field the wind wafts to my ears a
    shout of applause, (some special success,)
And ever the sound of the cannon far or near, (rousing even in dreams a
    devilish exultation and all the old mad joy in the depths of my
    soul,)
And ever the hastening of infantry shifting positions, batteries, cavalry,
    moving hither and thither,

---

* Entitled "The Veteran's Vision" in *Drum-Taps*.

(The falling, dying, I heed not, the wounded dripping and red I heed
    not, some to the rear are hobbling,)
Grime, heat, rush, aides-de-camp galloping by or on a full run,
With the patter of small arms, the warning *s-s-t* of the rifles, (these in my
    vision I hear or see,)
And bombs bursting in air, and at night the vari-color'd rockets.

1865   1881

Race of Veterans

Race of veterans — race of victors!
Race of the soil, ready for conflict — race of the conquering march!
(No more credulity's race, abiding-temper'd race,)
Race henceforth owning no law but the law of itself,
Race of passion and the storm.

1865–6   1871

O Tan-Faced Prairie-Boy

O tan-faced prairie-boy,
Before you came to camp came many a welcome gift,
Praises and presents came and nourishing food, till at last among the
    recruits,
You came, taciturn, with nothing to give — we but look'd on each other,
When lo! more than all the gifts of the world you gave me.

1865   1867

Look down Fair Moon

Look down fair moon and bathe this scene,
Pour softly down night's nimbus floods on faces ghastly, swollen, purple,
On the dead on their backs with arms toss'd wide,
Pour down your unstinted nimbus sacred moon.

1865   1867

Reconciliation

Word over all, beautiful as the sky,
Beautiful that war and all its deeds of carnage must in time be utterly
     lost,
That the hands of the sisters Death and Night incessantly softly wash
     again, and ever again, this soil'd world;
For my enemy is dead, a man divine as myself is dead,
I look where he lies white-faced and still in the coffin — I draw near,
Bend down and touch lightly with my lips the white face in the coffin.

1865–6   1881

To a Certain Civilian*

Did you ask dulcet rhymes from me?
Did you seek the civilian's peaceful and languishing rhymes?
Did you find what I sang erewhile so hard to follow?
Why I was not singing erewhile for you to follow, to understand — nor
     am I now;
(I have been born of the same as the war was born,
The drum-corps' rattle is ever to me sweet music, I love well the martial
     dirge,
With slow wail and convulsive throb leading the officer's funeral;)
What to such as you anyhow such a poet as I? therefore leave my works,
And go lull yourself with what you can understand, and with piano-
     tunes,
For I lull nobody, and you will never understand me.

1865   1871

---

* Entitled "Did You Ask Dulcet Rhymes from Me?" in *Drum-Taps*.

Spirit Whose Work Is Done

(Washington City, 1865)

Spirit whose work is done — spirit of dreadful hours!
Ere departing fade from my eyes your forests of bayonets;
Spirit of gloomiest fears and doubts, (yet onward ever unfaltering press-
    ing,)
Spirit of many a solemn day and many a savage scene — electric spirit,
That with muttering voice through the war now closed, like a tireless
    phantom flitted,
Rousing the land with breath of flame, while you beat and beat the
    drum,
Now as the sound of the drum, hollow and harsh to the last, reverberates
    round me,
As your ranks, your immortal ranks, return, return from the battles,
As the muskets of the young men yet lean over their shoulders,
As I look on the bayonets bristling over their shoulders,
As those slanted bayonets, whole forests of them appearing in the
    distance, approach and pass on, returning homeward,
Moving with steady motion, swaying to and fro to the right and left,
Evenly, lightly rising and falling while the steps keep time;
Spirit of hours I knew, all hectic red one day, but pale as death next day,
Touch my mouth ere you depart, press my lips close,
Leave me your pulses of rage — bequeath them to me — fill me with
    currents convulsive,
Let them scorch and blister out of my chants when you are gone,
Let them identify you to the future in these songs.

1865–6   *1881*

To the Leaven'd Soil They Trod

To the leaven'd soil they trod calling I sing for the last,
(Forth from my tent emerging for good, loosing, untying the tent-ropes,)
In the freshness the forenoon air, in the far-stretching circuits and vistas
    again to peace restored,
To the fiery fields emanative and the endless vistas beyond, to the South
    and the North,
To the leaven'd soil of the general Western world to attest my songs,
To the Alleghanian hills and the tireless Mississippi,

To the rocks I calling sing, and all the trees in the woods,
To the plains of the poems of heroes, to the prairies spreading wide,
To the far-off sea and the unseen winds, and the sane impalpable air;
And responding they answer all, (but not in words,)
The average earth, the witness of war and peace, acknowledges mutely,
The prairie draws me close, as the father to bosom broad the son,
The Northern ice and rain that began me nourish me to the end,
But the hot sun of the South is to fully ripen my songs.

1865–6   1881

When Lilacs Last in the Dooryard Bloom'd

1 When lilacs last in the dooryard bloom'd,
   And the great star early droop'd in the western sky in the night,
   I mourn'd, and yet shall mourn with ever-returning spring.

   Ever-returning spring, trinity sure to me you bring,
   Lilac blooming perennial and drooping star in the west,
   And thought of him I love.

2 O powerful western fallen star!
   O shades of night—O moody, tearful night!
   O great star disappear'd—O the black murk that hides the star!
   O cruel hands that hold me powerless—O helpless soul of me!
   O harsh surrounding cloud that will not free my soul.

3 In the dooryard fronting an old farm-house near the whitewash'd
        palings,
   Stands the lilac-bush tall-growing with heart-shaped leaves of rich
        green,
   With many a pointed blossom rising delicate, with the perfume
        strong I love,
   With every leaf a miracle—and from this bush in the dooryard,
   With delicate-color'd blossoms and heart-shaped leaves of rich green,
   A sprig with its flower I break.

4 In the swamp in secluded recesses,
   A shy and hidden bird is warbling a song.

   Solitary the thrush,
   The hermit withdrawn to himself, avoiding the settlements,
   Sings by himself a song.

Song of the bleeding throat,
Death's outlet song of life, (for well dear brother I know,
If thou wast not granted to sing thou would'st surely die.)

5 Over the breast of the spring, the land, amid cities,
   Amid lanes and through old woods, where lately the violets peep'd
        from the ground, spotting the gray debris,
   Amid the grass in the fields each side of the lanes, passing the endless
        grass,
   Passing the yellow-spear'd wheat, every grain from its shroud in the
        dark-brown fields uprisen,
   Passing the apple-tree blows of white and pink in the orchards,
   Carrying a corpse to where it shall rest in the grave,
   Night and day journeys a coffin.

6 Coffin that passes through lanes and streets,
   Through day and night with the great cloud darkening the land,
   With the pomp of the inloop'd flags with the cities draped in black,
   With the show of the States themselves as of crape-veil'd women
        standing,
   With processions long and winding and the flambeaus of the night,
   With the countless torches lit, with the silent sea of faces and the
        unbared heads,
   With the waiting depot, the arriving coffin, and the sombre faces,
   With dirges through the night, with the thousand voices rising strong
        and solemn,
   With all the mournful voices of the dirges pour'd around the coffin,
   The dim-lit churches and the shuddering organs — where amid these
        you journey,
   With the tolling tolling bells' perpetual clang,
   Here, coffin that slowly passes,
   I give you my sprig of lilac.

7 (Nor for you, for one alone,
   Blossoms and branches green to coffins all I bring,
   For fresh as the morning, thus would I chant a song for you O sane
        and sacred death.

   All over bouquets of roses,
   O death, I cover you over with roses and early lilies,
   But mostly and now the lilac that blooms the first,
   Copious I break, I break the sprigs from the bushes,
   With loaded arms I come, pouring for you,
   For you and the coffins all of you O death.)

8 O western orb sailing the heaven,
 Now I know what you must have meant as a month since I walk'd,
 As I walk'd in silence the transparent shadowy night,
 As I saw you had something to tell as you bent to me night after night,
 As you droop'd from the sky low down as if to my side, (while the other
     stars all look'd on,)
 As we wander'd together the solemn night, (for something I know not
     what kept me from sleep,)
 As the night advanced, and I saw on the rim of the west how full you
     were of woe,
 As I stood on the rising ground in the breeze in the cool transparent
     night,
 As I watch'd where you pass'd and was lost in the netherward black of
     the night,
 As my soul in its trouble dissatisfied sank, as where you sad orb,
 Concluded, dropt in the night, and was gone.

9 Sing on there in the swamp,
 O singer bashful and tender, I hear your notes, I hear your call,
 I hear, I come presently, I understand you,
 But a moment I linger, for the lustrous star has detain'd me,
 The star my departing comrade holds and detains me.

10 O how shall I warble myself for the dead one there I loved?
 And how shall I deck my song for the large sweet soul that has gone?
 And what shall my perfume be for the grave of him I love?

 Sea-winds blown from east and west,
 Blown from the Eastern sea and blown from the Western sea, till
     there on the prairies meeting,
 These and with these and the breath of my chant,
 I'll perfume the grave of him I love.

11 O what shall I hang on the chamber walls?
 And what shall the pictures be that I hang on the walls,
 To adorn the burial-house of him I love?

 Pictures of growing spring and farms and homes,
 With the Fourth-month eve at sundown, and the gray smoke lucid
     and bright,
 With floods of the yellow gold of the gorgeous, indolent, sinking sun,
     burning, expanding the air,
 With the fresh sweet herbage under foot, and the pale green leaves
     of the trees prolific,

In the distance the flowing glaze, the breast of the river, with a wind-
    dapple here and there,
With ranging hills on the banks, with many a line against the sky,
    and shadows,
And the city at hand with dwellings so dense, and stacks of chim-
    neys,
And all the scenes of life and the workshops, and the workmen
    homeward returning.

12 Lo, body and soul — this land,
    My own Manhattan with spires, and the sparkling and hurrying
        tides, and the ships,
    The varied and ample land, the South and the North in the light,
        Ohio's shores and flashing Missouri,
    And ever the far-spreading prairies cover'd with grass and corn.

    Lo, the most excellent sun so calm and haughty,
    The violet and purple morn with just-felt breezes,
    The gentle soft-born measureless light,
    The miracle spreading bathing all, the fulfill'd noon,
    The coming eve delicious, the welcome night and the stars,
    Over my cities shining all, enveloping man and land.

13 Sing on, sing on you gray-brown bird,
    Sing from the swamps, the recesses, pour your chant from the
        bushes,
    Limitless out of the dusk, out of the cedars and pines.

    Sing on dearest brother, warble your reedy song,
    Loud human song, with voice of uttermost woe.

    O liquid and free and tender!
    O wild and loose to my soul — O wondrous singer!
    You only I hear — yet the star holds me, (but will soon depart,)
    Yet the lilac with mastering odor holds me.

14 Now while I sat in the day and look'd forth,
    In the close of the day with its light and the fields of spring, and the
        farmers preparing their crops,
    In the large unconscious scenery of my land with its lakes and
        forests,
    In the heavenly aerial beauty, (after the perturb'd winds and the
        storms,)
    Under the arching heavens of the afternoon swift passing, and the
        voices of children and women,

The many-moving sea-tides, and I saw the ships how they sail'd,
And the summer approaching with richness, and the fields all busy
      with labor,
And the infinite separate houses, how they all went on, each with its
      meals and minutia of daily usages,
And the streets how their throbbings throbb'd, and the cities pent —
      lo, then and there,
Falling upon them all and among them all, enveloping me with the
      rest,
Appear'd the cloud, appear'd the long black trail,
And I knew death, its thought, and the sacred knowledge of
      death.

Then with the knowledge of death as walking one side of me,
And the thought of death close-walking the other side of me,
And I in the middle as with companions, and as holding the hands of
      companions,
I fled forth to the hiding receiving night that talks not,
Down to the shores of the water, the path by the swamp in the
      dimness,
To the solemn shadowy cedars and ghostly pines so still.

And the singer so shy to the rest receiv'd me,
The gray-brown bird I know receiv'd us comrades three,
And he sang the carol of death, and a verse for him I love.

From deep secluded recesses,
From the fragrant cedars and the ghostly pines so still,
Came the carol of the bird.

And the charm of the carol rapt me,
As I held as if by their hands my comrades in the night,
And the voice of my spirit tallied the song of the bird.

Come lovely and soothing death,
Undulate round the world, serenely arriving, arriving,
In the day, in the night, to all, to each,
Sooner or later delicate death.

Prais'd be the fathomless universe,
For life and joy, and for objects and knowledge curious,
And for love, sweet love — but praise! praise! praise!
For the sure-enwinding arms of cool-enfolding death.

Dark mother always gliding near with soft feet,
Have none chanted for thee a chant of fullest welcome?
Then I chant it for thee, I glorify thee above all,
I bring thee a song that when thou must indeed come, come un-
  falteringly.

Approach strong deliveress,
When it is so, when thou hast taken them I joyously sing the dead,
Lost in the loving floating ocean of thee,
Laved in the flood of thy bliss O death.

From me to thee glad serenades,
Dances for thee I propose saluting thee, adornments and feastings for
  thee,
And the sights of the open landscape and the high-spread sky are
  fitting,
And life and the fields, and the huge and thoughtful night.

The night in silence under many a star,
The ocean shore and the husky whispering wave whose voice I know,
And the soul turning to thee O vast and well-veil'd death,
And the body gratefully nestling close to thee.

Over the tree-tops I float thee a song,
Over the rising and sinking waves, over the myriad fields and the
  prairies wide,
Over the dense-pack'd cities all and the teeming wharves and ways,
I float this carol with joy, with joy to thee O death.

15 To the tally of my soul,
    Loud and strong kept up the gray-brown bird,
    With pure deliberate notes spreading filling the night.

    Loud in the pines and cedars dim,
    Clear in the freshness moist and the swamp-perfume,
    And I with my comrades there in the night.

    While my sight that was bound in my eyes unclosed,
    As to long panoramas of visions.

    And I saw askant the armies,
    I saw as in noiseless dreams hundreds of battle-flags,
    Borne through the smoke of the battles and pierc'd with missiles I
      saw them,
    And carried hither and yon through the smoke, and torn and bloody,

And at last but a few shreds left on the staffs, (and all in silence,)
And the staffs all splinter'd and broken.

I saw battle-corpses, myriads of them,
And the white skeletons of young men, I saw them,
I saw the debris and debris of all the slain soldiers of the war,
But I saw they were not as was thought,
They themselves were fully at rest, they suffer'd not,
The living remain'd and suffer'd, the mother suffer'd,
And the wife and the child and the musing comrade suffer'd,
And the armies that remain'd suffer'd.

16 Passing the visions, passing the night,
Passing, unloosing the hold of my comrades' hands,
Passing the song of the hermit bird and the tallying song of my soul,
Victorious song, death's outlet song, yet varying ever-altering song,
As low and wailing, yet clear the notes, rising and falling, flooding
        the night,
Sadly sinking and fainting, as warning and warning, and yet again
        bursting with joy,
Covering the earth and filling the spread of the heaven,
As that powerful psalm in the night I heard from recesses,
Passing, I leave thee lilac with heart-shaped leaves,
I leave thee there in the dooryard, blooming, returning with spring.

I cease from my song for thee,
From my gaze on thee in the west, fronting the west, communing
        with thee,
O comrade lustrous with silver face in the night.

Yet each to keep and all, retrievements out of the night,
The song, the wondrous chant of the gray-brown bird,
And the tallying chant, the echo arous'd in my soul,
With the lustrous and drooping star with the countenance full of woe,
With the holders holding my hand nearing the call of the bird,
Comrades mine and I in the midst, and their memory ever to keep,
        for the dead I loved so well,
For the sweetest, wisest soul of all my days and lands — and this for
        his dear sake,
Lilac and star and bird twined with the chant of my soul,
There in the fragrant pines and the cedars dusk and dim.

1865–6   1881

O Captain! My Captain!

O Captain! my Captain! our fearful trip is done,
The ship has weather'd every rack, the prize we sought is won,
The port is near, the bells I hear, the people all exulting,
While follow eyes the steady keel, the vessel grim and daring;
        But O heart! heart! heart!
      O the bleeding drops of red,
          Where on the deck my Captain lies,
            Fallen cold and dead.

O Captain! my Captain! rise up and hear the bells;
Rise up — for you the flag is flung — for you the bugle trills,
For you bouquets and ribbon'd wreaths — for you the shores a-crowding,
For you they call, the swaying mass, their eager faces turning;
        Here Captain! dear father!
        The arm beneath your head!
          It is some dream that on the deck,
            You've fallen cold and dead.

My Captain does not answer, his lips are pale and still,
My father does not feel my arm, he has no pulse nor will,
The ship is anchor'd safe and sound, its voyage closed and done,
From fearful trip the victor ship comes in with object won:
        Exult O shores, and ring O bells!
        But I with mournful tread,
          Walk the deck my Captain lies,
            Fallen cold and dead.

1865   1871

Hush'd Be the Camps To-Day

(May 4, 1865)

Hush'd be the camps to-day,
And soldiers let us drape our war-worn weapons,
And each with musing soul retire to celebrate,
Our dear commander's death.

No more for him life's stormy conflicts,
Nor victory, nor defeat — no more time's dark events,
Charging like ceaseless clouds across the sky.

But sing poet in our name,
Sing of the love we bore him — because you — dweller in camps, know it
    truly.

As they invault the coffin there,
Sing — as they close the doors of earth upon him — one verse,
For the heavy hearts of soldiers.

1865   *1871*

This Dust Was Once the Man

This dust was once the man,
Gentle, plain, just and resolute, under whose cautious hand,
Against the foulest crime in history known in any land or age,
Was saved the Union of these States.

1871   *1871*

Quicksand Years

Quicksand years that whirl me I know not whither,
Your schemes, politics, fail, lines give way, substances mock and elude
    me,
Only the theme I sing, the great and strong-possess'd soul, eludes not,
One's-self must never give way — that is the final substance — that out of
    all is sure,
Out of politics, triumphs, battles, life, what at last finally remains?
When shows break up what but One's-Self is sure?

1865   *1871*

Old War-Dreams*

In midnight sleep of many a face of anguish,
Of the look at first of the mortally wounded, (of that indescribable look,)
Of the dead on their backs with arms extended wide,
       I dream, I dream, I dream.

Of scenes of Nature, fields and mountains,
Of skies so beauteous after a storm, and at night the moon so unearthly
    bright,
Shining sweetly, shining down, where we dig the trenches and gather
    the heaps,
       I dream, I dream, I dream.

Long have they pass'd, faces and trenches and fields,
Where through the carnage I moved with a callous composure, or away
    from the fallen,
Onward I sped at the time — but now of their forms at night,
       I dream, I dream, I dream.

1865–6   *1881*

Ashes of Soldiers†

Ashes of soldiers South or North,
As I muse retrospective murmuring a chant in thought,
The war resumes, again to my sense your shapes,
And again the advance of the armies.

Noiseless as mists and vapors,
From their graves in the trenches ascending,
From cemeteries all through Virginia and Tennessee,
From every point of the compass out of the countless graves,

---

* Entitled "In Clóuds Descending, in Midnight Sleep" in *Sequel to Drum-Taps*.
† Entitled "Hymn of Dead Soldiers" in *Drum-Taps*.

In wafted clouds, in myriads large, or squads of twos or threes or single
      ones they come,
And silently gather round me.

Now sound no note O trumpeters,
Not at the head of my cavalry parading on spirited horses,
With sabres drawn and glistening, and carbines by their thighs, (ah my
      brave horsemen!
My handsome tan-faced horsemen! what life, what joy and pride,
With all the perils were yours.)

Nor you drummers, neither at reveillé at dawn,
Nor the long roll alarming the camp, nor even the muffled beat for a
      burial,
Nothing from you this time O drummers bearing my warlike drums.

But aside from these and the marts of wealth and the crowded prom-
      enade,
Admitting around me comrades close unseen by the rest and voice-
      less,
The slain elate and alive again, the dust and debris alive,
I chant this chant of my silent soul in the name of all dead soldiers.

Faces so pale with wondrous eyes, very dear, gather closer yet,
Draw close, but speak not.

Phantoms of countless lost,
Invisible to the rest henceforth become my companions,
Follow me ever — desert me not while I live.

Sweet are the blooming cheeks of the living — sweet are the musical
      voices sounding,
But sweet, ah sweet, are the dead with their silent eyes.

Dearest comrades, all is over and long gone,
But love is not over — and what love, O comrades!
Perfume from battle-fields rising, up from the fœtor arising.

Perfume therefore my chant, O love, immortal love,
Give me to bathe the memories of all dead soldiers,
Shroud them, embalm them, cover them all over with tender pride.

Perfume all — make all wholesome,
Make these ashes to nourish and blossom,
O love, solve all, fructify all with the last chemistry.

Give me exhaustless, make me a fountain,
That I exhale love from me wherever I go like a moist perennial dew,
For the ashes of all dead soldiers South or North.

1865   *1881*

Pensive on Her Dead Gazing

Pensive on her dead gazing I heard the Mother of All,
Desperate on the torn bodies, on the forms covering the battle-fields
    gazing,
(As the last gun ceased, but the scent of the powder-smoke linger'd,)
As she call'd to her earth with mournful voice while she stalk'd,
Absorb them well O my earth, she cried, I charge you lose not my sons,
    lose not an atom,
And you streams absorb them well, taking their dear blood,
And you local spots, and you airs that swim above lightly impalpable,
And all you essences of soil and growth, and you my rivers' depths,
And you mountain sides, and the woods where my dear children's blood
    trickling redden'd,
And you trees down in your roots to bequeath to all future trees,
My dead absorb or South or North — my young men's bodies absorb,
    and their precious precious blood,
Which holding in trust for me faithfully back again give me many a year
    hence,
In unseen essence and odor of surface and grass, centuries hence,
In blowing airs from the fields back again give me my darlings, give my
    immortal heroes,
Exhale me them centuries hence, breathe me their breath, let not an
    atom be lost,
O years and graves! O air and soil! O my dead, an aroma sweet!
Exhale them perennial sweet death, years, centuries hence.

1865   *1881*

Camps of Green

Not alone those camps of white, old comrades of the wars,
When as order'd forward, after a long march,
Footsore and weary, soon as the light lessens we halt for the night,
Some of us so fatigued carrying the gun and knapsack, dropping asleep
    in our tracks,
Others pitching the little tents, and the fires lit up begin to sparkle,
Outposts of pickets posted surrounding alert through the dark,
And a word provided for countersign, careful for safety,
Till to the call of the drummers at daybreak loudly beating the drums,
We rise up refresh'd, the night and sleep pass'd over, and resume our
    journey,
Or proceed to battle.

Lo, the camps of the tents of green,
Which the days of peace keep filling, and the days of war keep filling,
With a mystic army, (is it too order'd forward? is it too only halting
    awhile,
Till night and sleep pass over?)

Now in those camps of green, in their tents dotting the world,
In the parents, children, husbands, wives, in them, in the old and young,
Sleeping under the sunlight, sleeping under the moonlight, content and
    silent there at last,
Behold the mighty bivouac-field and waiting-camp of all,
Of the corps and generals all, and the President over the corps and
    generals all,
And of each of us O soldiers, and of each and all in the ranks we fought,
(There without hatred we all, all meet.)

For presently O soldiers, we too camp in our place in the bivouac-camps
    of green,
But we need not provide for outposts, nor word for the countersign,
Nor drummer to beat the morning drum.

1865   *1881*

POEMS NOT INCLUDED IN THE 1891–92 *LEAVES OF GRASS*

Bathed in War's Perfume

Bathed in war's perfume—delicate flag!
O to hear you call the sailors and the soldiers! flag like a beautiful
    woman!
O to hear the tramp, tramp, of a million answering men! O the ships
    they arm with joy!
O to see you leap and beckon from the tall masts of ships!
O to see you peering down on the sailors on the decks!
Flag like the eyes of women.

1865   1876

Solid, Ironical, Rolling Orb

Solid, ironical, rolling orb!
Master of all, and matter of fact!—at last I accept your terms;
Bringing to practical, vulgar tests, of all my ideal dreams,
And of me, as lover and hero.

1865   1876

SELECTIONS FROM *MEMORANDA*
DURING THE WAR (1875–76)[1]

Falmouth, Va., opposite Fredericksburgh, December 21, 1862. —
Began my visits among the Camp Hospitals in the Army of the Potomac.
Spent a good part of the day in a large brick mansion, on the banks of the
Rappahannock, used as a Hospital since the battle — Seems to have
receiv'd only the worst cases. Out doors, at the foot of a tree, within ten
yards of the front of the house, I notice a heap of amputated feet, legs,
arms, hands, &c., a full load for a one-horse cart. Several dead bodies lie
near, each cover'd with its brown woollen blanket. In the door-yard,
towards the river, are fresh graves, mostly of officers, their names on
pieces of barrel-staves or broken board, stuck in the dirt. (Most of these
bodies were subsequently taken up and transported North to their
friends.). . . . . The large mansion is quite crowded, upstairs and
down, everything impromptu, no system, all bad enough, but I have no
doubt the best that can be done; all the wounds pretty bad, some
frightful, the men in their old clothes, unclean and bloody. Some of
the wounded are rebel soldiers and officers, prisoners. One, a
Mississippian — a captain — hit badly in leg, I talk'd with some time; he
ask'd me for papers, which I gave him. (I saw him three months after-
ward in Washington, with his leg amputated, doing well.)[2]. I
went through the rooms, downstairs and up. Some of the men were
dying. I had nothing to give at that visit, but wrote a few letters to folks
home, mothers, &c. Also talk'd to three or four, who seem'd most
susceptible to it, and needing it.

(Everything is quiet now, here about Falmouth and the Rappahan-
nock, but there was noise enough a week or so ago. Probably the earth
never shook by artificial means, nor the air reverberated, more than on
that winter daybreak of eight or nine days since, when Gen. Burnside
order'd all the batteries of the army to combine for the bombardment of
Fredericksburgh. It was in its way the most magnificent and terrible

---

1. Most of Whitman's *Memoranda* was incorporated (slightly revised) in his *Specimen Days & Collect* (1882–83).

2. *a Mississippian . . . doing well*] Whitman refers to this soldier in his letter to Nat Bloom and Fred Gray, March 19, 1863 (see page 62).

spectacle, with all the adjunct of sound, throughout the War. The perfect hush of the just-ending night was suddenly broken by the first gun, and in an instant all the thunderers, big and little, were in full chorus, which they kept up without intermission for several hours.)

December 23 to 31. — The results of the late battles are exhibited everywhere about here in thousands of cases, (hundreds die every day,) in the Camp, Brigade, and Division Hospitals. These are merely tents, and sometimes very poor ones, the wounded lying on the ground, lucky if their blankets are spread on layers of pine or hemlock twigs or small leaves. No cots; seldom even a mattress. It is pretty cold. The ground is frozen hard, and there is occasional snow. I go around from one case to another. I do not see that I do much good, but I cannot leave them. Once in a while some youngster holds on to me convulsively, and I do what I can for him; at any rate, stop with him and sit near him for hours, if he wishes it.

Besides the hospitals, I also go occasionally on long tours through the camps, talking with the men, &c. Sometimes at night among the groups around the fires, in their shebang enclosures of bushes. These are curious shows, full of characters and groups. I soon get acquainted anywhere in camp, with officers or men, and am always well used. Sometimes I go down on picket with the regiments I know best. . . . . . . As to rations, the army here at present seems to be tolerably well supplied, and the men have enough, such as it is, mainly salt pork and hard tack. Most of the regiments lodge in the flimsy little shelter-tents. A few have built themselves huts of logs and mud, with fireplaces.

Fifty Hours Left Wounded on the Field. — Here is a case of a soldier I found among the crowded cots in the Patent Office.[3] He likes to have some one to talk to, and we will listen to him. He got badly hit in his leg and side at Fredericksburgh that eventful Saturday, 13th of December. He lay the succeeding two days and nights helpless on the field, between the city and those grim terraces of batteries; his company and regiment had been compell'd to leave him to his fate. To make matters worse, it happen'd he lay with his head slightly down hill, and could not help himself. At the end of some fifty hours he was brought off, with other wounded, under a flag of truce. . . . . I ask him how the rebels treated him as he lay during those two days and nights within reach of them — whether they came to him — whether they abused him? He answers that several of the rebels, soldiers and others, came to him, at one time and another. A couple of them, who were together, spoke roughly and sarcastically, but nothing worse. One middle-aged man, however, who seem'd to be moving around the field, among the dead and wounded, for benevolent purposes, came to him in a way he will

_____

3. *Patent Office*] The Patent Office was converted to a military hospital during the War

never forget; treated our soldier kindly, bound up his wounds, cheer'd him, gave him a couple of biscuits, and a drink of whiskey and water; ask'd him if he could eat some beef. This good Secesh, however, did not change our soldier's position, for it might have caused the blood to burst from the wounds, clotted and stagnated. Our soldier is from Pennsylvania; has had a pretty severe time; the wounds proved to be bad ones. But he retains a good heart, and is at present on the gain. . . . . (It is not uncommon for the men to remain on the field this way, one, two, or even four or five days.)

Wednesday, Feb. 4th. — Visited Armory Square Hospital, went pretty thoroughly through Wards E and D. Supplied paper and envelopes to all who wish'd — as usual, found plenty of the men who needed those articles. Wrote letters. Saw and talk'd with two or three members of the Brooklyn Fourteenth. . . . . A poor fellow in Ward D, with a fearful wound in a fearful condition, was having some loose splinters of bone taken from the neighborhood of the wound. The operation was long, and one of great pain — yet, after it was well commenced, the soldier bore it in silence. He sat up, propp'd — was much wasted — had lain a long time quiet in one position, (not for days only, but weeks,) — a bloodless, brown-skinn'd face, with eyes full of determination — belong'd to a New York regiment. There was an unusual cluster of surgeons, medical cadets, nurses, &c., around his bed — I thought the whole thing was done with tenderness, and done well.

In one case, the wife sat by the side of her husband, his sickness, typhoid fever, pretty bad. In another, by the side of her son — a mother — she told me she had seven children, and this was the youngest. (A fine, kind, healthy, gentle mother, good-looking, not very old, with a cap on her head, and dress'd like home — what a charm it gave to the whole Ward.) I liked the woman nurse in Ward E — I noticed how she sat a long time by a poor fellow who just had, that morning, in addition to his other sickness, bad hemmorhage — she gently assisted him, reliev'd him of the blood, holding a cloth to his mouth, as he cough'd it up — he was so weak he could only just turn his head over on the pillow.

One young New York man, with a bright, handsome face, had been lying several months from a most disagreeable wound, receiv'd at Bull Run. A bullet had shot him right through the bladder, hitting him front, low in the belly, and coming out back. He had suffer'd much — the water came out of the wound, by slow but steady quantities, for many weeks — so that he lay almost constantly in a sort of puddle — and there were other disagreeable circumstances. He was of good heart, however. At present comparatively comfortable; had a bad throat, was delighted with a stick of horehound candy I gave him, with one or two other trifles.

The White House, by Moonlight — Feb. 24. — A spell of fine soft weather. I wander about a good deal, especially at night, under the moon. To-night took a long look at the President's House — and here is my splurge about it. The white portico — the brilliant gas-light shining — the palace-like portico — the tall, round columns, spotless as snow — the walls also — the tender and soft moonlight, flooding the pale marble, and making peculiar faint languishing shades, not shadows — everywhere too a soft transparent haze, a thin blue moon-lace, hanging in the night in the air — the brilliant and extra plentiful clusters of gas, on and around the facade, columns, portico, &c. — everything so white, so marbly pure and dazzling, yet soft — the White House of future poems, and of dreams and dramas, there in the soft and copious moon — the pure and gorgeous front, in the trees, under the night-lights, under the lustrous flooding moon, full of reality, full of illusion — The forms of the trees, leafless, silent, in trunk and myriad-angles of branches, under the stars and sky — the White House of the land, the White House of the night, and of beauty and silence — sentries at the gates, and by the portico, silent, pacing there in blue overcoats — stopping you not at all, but eyeing you with sharp eyes, whichever way you move.

A Connecticut Case. — This young man in bed 25[4] is H. D. B., of the Twenty-seventh Connecticut, Company B. His folks live at Northford, near New Haven. Though not more than twenty-one, or thereabouts, he has knock'd much around the world, on sea and land, and has seen some fighting on both. When I first saw him he was very sick, with no appetite. He declined offers of money — said he did not need anything. As I was quite anxious to do something, he confess'd that he had a hankering for a good home-made rice pudding — thought he could relish it better than anything. At this time his stomach was very weak. (The doctor, whom I consulted, said nourishment would do him more good than anything; but things in the hospital, though better than usual, revolted him.) I soon procured B. his rice-pudding. A Washington lady, (Mrs. O'C.), hearing his wish, made the pudding herself, and I took it up to him the next day. He subsequently told me he lived upon it for three or four days. . . . . . . This B. is a good sample of the American Eastern young man — the typical Yankee. I took a fancy to him, and gave him a nice pipe, for a keepsake. He receiv'd afterwards a box of things from home, and nothing would do but I must take dinner with him, which I did, and a very good one it was.

Two Brooklyn Boys. — Here in this same Ward are two young men from Brooklyn, members of the Fifty-first New York. I had known

---

4. *bed 25*] In this and the following entry, Whitman describes some of the patients at Campbell Hospital, a "collection of barrack-like one-story edifices . . . on Seventh Street" in Washington.

both the two as young lads at home, so they seem near to me. One of them, J. L., lies there with an amputated arm, the stump healing pretty well. (I saw him lying on the ground at Fredericksburgh last December, all bloody, just after the arm was taken off. He was very phlegmatic about it, munching away at a cracker in the remaining hand — made no fuss.) He will recover, and thinks and talks yet of meeting the Johnny Rebs.

June 18. — In one of the Hospitals I find Thomas Haley, Co. M, Fourth New York Cavalry — a regular Irish boy, a fine specimen of youthful physical manliness — shot through the lungs — inevitably dying — came over to this country from Ireland to enlist — has not a single friend or acquaintance here — is sleeping soundly at this moment, (but it is the sleep of death) — has a bullet-hole straight through the lung. . . . . . . I saw Tom when first brought here, three days since, and didn't suppose he could live twelve hours — (yet he looks well enough in the face to a casual observer.) He lies there with his frame exposed above the waist, all naked, for coolness, a fine built man, the tan not yet bleach'd from his cheeks and neck. It is useless to talk to him, as with his sad hurt, and the stimulants they give him, and the utter strangeness of every object, face, furniture, &c., the poor fellow, even when awake, is like a frighten'd, shy animal. Much of the time he sleeps, or half sleeps. (Sometimes I thought he knew more than he show'd.) I often come and sit by him in perfect silence; he will breathe for ten minutes as softly and evenly as a young babe asleep. Poor youth, so handsome, athletic, with profuse beautiful shining hair. One time as I sat looking at him while he lay asleep, he suddenly, without the least start, awaken'd, open'd his eyes, gave me a long, long steady look, turning his face very slightly to gaze easier — one long, clear silent look — a slight sigh — then turn'd back and went into his doze again. Little he knew, poor death-stricken boy, the heart of the stranger that hover'd near.

Bad Wounds, the Young. — The soldiers are nearly all young men, and far more American than is generally supposed — I should say ninetenths are native-born. Among the arrivals from Chancellorsville I find a large proportion of Ohio, Indiana, and Illinois men. As usual, there are all sorts of wounds. Some of the men fearfully burnt from the explosion of artillery caissons. One Ward has a long row of officers, some with ugly hurts. Yesterday was perhaps worse than usual. Amputations are going on — the attendants are dressing wounds. As you pass by, you must be on your guard where you look. I saw the other day a gentleman, a visitor apparently from curiosity, in one of the Wards, stop and turn a moment to look at an awful wound they were probing, &c. He turn'd pale, and in a moment more he had fainted away and fallen on the floor.

A New York Soldier. — This afternoon, July 22, I have spent a long time with Oscar F. Wilber, Company G, One Hundred and Fifty-fourth New York, low with chronic diarrhœa, and a bad wound also. He ask'd me to read to him a chapter in the New Testament. I complied, and ask'd him what I should read. He said: "Make your own choice." I open'd at the close of one of the first books of the Evangelists, and read the chapters describing the latter hours of Christ, and the scenes at the crucifixion. The poor, wasted young man ask'd me to read the following chapter also, how Christ rose again. I read very slowly, for Oscar was feeble. It pleas'd him very much, yet the tears were in his eyes. He ask'd me if I enjoy'd religion. I said: "Perhaps not, my dear, in the way you mean, and yet, may-be, it is the same thing." He said: "It is my chief reliance." He talk'd of death, and said he did not fear it. I said: "Why, Oscar, don't you think you will get well?" He said: "I may, but it is not probable." He spoke calmly of his condition. The wound was very bad; it discharg'd much. Then the diarrhœa had prostrated him, and I felt that he was even then the same as dying. He behaved very manly and affectionate. The kiss I gave him as I was about leaving he return'd fourfold. He gave me his mother's address, Mrs. Sally D. Wilber, Alleghany Post-office, Cattaraugus County, N. Y. I had several such interviews with him. He died a few days after the one just described.

Aug. 12. — I see the President almost every day, as I happen to live where he passes to or from his lodgings out of town. He never sleeps at the White House during the hot season, but has quarters at a healthy location, some three miles north of the city, the Soldiers' Home, a United States military establishment. I saw him this morning about 8½ coming in to business, riding on Vermont avenue, near L street. The sight is a significant one, (and different enough from how and where I first saw him.*) He always has a company of twenty-five or thirty cavalry, with sabres drawn, and held upright over their shoulders. The party makes no great show in uniforms or horses. Mr. Lincoln, on the saddle, generally rides a good-sized easy-going gray horse, is dress'd in plain

---

* I shall not easily forget the first time I saw Abraham Lincoln. It must have been about the 18th or 19th of February, 1861. It was rather a pleasant spring afternoon, in New York city, as Lincoln arrived there from the West to stop a few hours and then pass on to Washington, to prepare for his inauguration. I saw him in Broadway, near the site of the present Post-office. He had come down, I think, from Canal street, to stop at the Astor House. The broad spaces, sidewalks, and street in the neighborhood, and for some distance, were crowded with solid masses of people, many thousands. The omnibuses and other vehicles had been all turn'd off, leaving an unusual hush in that busy part of the city. Presently two or three shabby hack barouches made their way with some difficulty through the crowd, and drew up at the Astor House entrance. A tall figure step'd out of the centre of these barouches, paus'd leisurely on the sidewalk, look'd up at the dark

black, somewhat rusty and dusty; wears a black stiff hat, and looks about as ordinary in attire, &c., as the commonest man. A Lieutenant, with yellow straps, rides at his left, and following behind, two by two, come the cavalry men in their yellow-striped jackets. They are generally going at a slow trot, as that is the pace set them by the One they wait upon. The sabres and accoutrements clank, and the entirely unornamental *cortege* as it trots towards Lafayette square, arouses no sensation, only some curious stranger stops and gazes. I see very plainly ABRAHAM LINCOLN'S dark brown face, with the deep cut lines, the eyes, &c., always to me with a deep latent sadness in the expression. We have got so that we always exchange bows, and very cordial ones.

Sometimes the President goes and comes in an open barouche. The cavalry always accompany him, with drawn sabres. Often I notice as he goes out evenings — and sometimes in the morning, when he returns early — he turns off and halts at the large and handsome residence of the Secretary of War, on K street, and holds conference there. If in his barouche, I can see from my window he does not alight, but sits in the vehicle, and Mr. Stanton comes out to attend him. Sometimes one of his sons, a boy of ten or twelve, accompanies him, riding at his right on a pony.

Earlier in the summer I occasionally saw the President and his wife, toward the latter part of the afternoon, out in a barouche, on a pleasure ride through the city. Mrs. Lincoln was dress'd in complete black, with a long crape veil. The equipage is of the plainest kind, only two horses, and they nothing extra. They pass'd me once very close, and I saw the President in the face fully, as they were moving slow, and his look,

---

granite walls and looming architecture of the grand old hotel — then, after a relieving stretch of arms and legs, turn'd round for over a minute to slowly and good-humoredly scan the appearance of the vast and silent crowds — and so, with very moderate pace, and accompanied by a few unknown-looking persons, ascended the portico steps.

The figure, the look, the gait, are distinctly impress'd upon me yet; the unusual and uncouth height, the dress of complete black, the stovepipe hat push'd back on the head, the dark-brown complexion, the seam'd and wrinkled yet canny-looking face, the black, bushy head of hair, the disproportionately long neck, and the hands held behind as he stood observing the people. All was comparative and ominous silence. The new comer look'd with curiosity upon that immense sea of faces, and the sea of faces return'd the look with similar curiosity. In both there was a dash of something almost comical. Yet there was much anxiety in certain quarters. Cautious persons had fear'd that there would be some outbreak, some mark'd indignity or insult to the President elect on his passage through the city, for he possess'd no personal popularity in New York, and not much political. No such outbreak or insult, however, occurr'd. Only the silence of the crowd was very significant to those who were accustom'd to the usual demonstrations of New York in wild, tumultuous hurrahs — the deafening tumults of welcome, and the thunder-shouts of pack'd myriads along the whole line of Broadway, receiving Hungarian Kossuth or Filibuster Walker. [Whitman's note.]

though abstracted, happen'd to be directed steadily in my eye. He bow'd and smiled, but far beneath his smile I noticed well the expression I have alluded to. None of the artists or pictures have caught the deep, though subtle and indirect expression of this man's face. There is something else there. One of the great portrait painters of two or three centuries ago is needed.

Virginia.[5] — Dilapidated, fenceless, and trodden with war as Virginia is, wherever I move across her surface, I find myself rous'd to surprise and admiration. What capacity for products, improvements, human life, nourishment and expansion! Everywhere that I have been in the Old Dominion, (the subtle mockery of that title now!) such thoughts have fill'd me. The soil is yet far above the average of any of the northern States. And how full of breadth is the scenery, everywhere with distant mountains, everywhere convenient rivers. Even yet prodigal in forest woods, and surely eligible for all the fruits, orchards, and flowers. The skies and atmosphere most luscious, as I feel certain, from more than a year's residence in the State, and movements hither and yon. I should say very healthy, as a general thing. Then a rich and elastic quality, by night and by day. The sun rejoices in his strength, dazzling and burning, and yet, to me, never unpleasantly weakening. It is not the panting tropical heat, but invigorates. The north tempers it. The nights are often unsurpassable. Last evening (Feb. 8,) I saw the first of the new moon, the old moon clear along with it; the sky and air so clear, such transparent hues of color, it seem'd to me I had never really seen the new moon before. It was the thinnest cut crescent possible. It hung delicate just above the sulky shadow of the Blue Mountains. Ah, if it might prove an omen and good prophecy for this unhappy State.

An Incident.[6] — In one of the fights before Atlanta, a rebel soldier, of large size, evidently a young man, was mortally wounded in top of the head, so that the brains partially exuded. He lived three days, lying on his back on the spot where he first dropt. He dug with his heel in the ground during that time a hole big enough to put in a couple of ordinary knapsacks. He just lay there in the open air, and with little intermission kept his heel going night and day. Some of our soldiers then moved him to a house, but he died in a few minutes.

Another. — After the battles at Columbia, Tennessee, where we repuls'd about a score of vehement rebel charges, they left a great many wounded on the ground, mostly within our range. Whenever any of these wounded attempted to move away by any means, generally by

---

5. *Virginia*] In February 1864, Whitman traveled to Culpepper, Virginia, where he stayed "pretty well down toward the extreme front" of the fighting.

6. *An Incident*] Whitman was back in Washington in the summer of 1864, when this entry was written.

crawling off, our men without exception, brought them down by a bullet. They let none crawl away, no matter what his condition.

Deserters — Saturday, Oct. 24. — Saw a large squad of our own deserters, (over 300) surrounded with a strong cordon of arm'd guards, marching along Pennsylvania avenue. The most motley collection I ever saw, all sorts of rig, all sorts of hats and caps, many fine-looking young fellows, some of them shame-faced, some sickly, most of them dirty, shirts very dirty and long worn, &c. They tramp'd along without order, a huge huddling mass, not in ranks. I saw some of the spectators laughing, but I felt like anything else but laughing.

These deserters are far more numerous than would be thought. Almost every day I see squads of them, sometimes two or three at a time, with a small guard; sometimes ten or twelve, under a larger one. (I hear that desertions from the army now in the field have often averaged 10,000 a month. One of the commonest sights in Washington is a squad of deserters. I often think it curious that the military and civil operations do not clash, but they never do here.)

A Glimpse of War's Hell-Scenes. — In one of the late movements of our troops in the Valley, (near Upperville, I think,) a strong force of Moseby's mounted guerillas attack'd a train of wounded, and the guard of cavalry convoying them. The ambulances contain'd about 60 wounded, quite a number of them officers of rank. The rebels were in strength, and the capture of the train and its partial guard after a short snap was effectually accomplish'd.

No sooner had our men surrender'd, the rebels instantly commenced robbing the train, and murdering their prisoners, even the wounded. Here is the scene, or a sample of it, ten minutes after. Among the wounded officers in the ambulances were one, a Lieutenant of regulars, and another of higher rank. These two were dragg'd out on the ground on their backs, and were now surrounded by the guerillas, a demoniac crowd, each member of which was stabbing them in different parts of their bodies. One of the officers had his feet pinn'd firmly to the ground by bayonets stuck through them and thrust into the ground. These two officers, as afterwards found on examination, had receiv'd about twenty such thrusts, some of them through the mouth, face, &c. The wounded had all been dragg'd (to give a better chance also for plunder,) out of their wagons; some had been effectually dispatch'd, and their bodies lying there lifeless and bloody. Others, not yet dead, but horribly mutilated, were moaning or groaning. Of our men who surrender'd, most had been thus maim'd or slaughter'd.

At this instant a force of our cavalry, who had been following the train at some interval, charged suddenly upon the Secesh captors, who proceeded at once to make the best escape they could. Most of them got away, but we gobbled two officers and seventeen men, as it were in the very acts just described. The sight was one which admitted of little discussion, as may be imagined. The seventeen captured men and two officers were put under guard for the night, but it was decided there and then that they should die.

The next morning the two officers were taken in the town, separate places, put in the centre of the street, and shot. The seventeen men were taken to an open ground, a little to one side. They were placed in a hollow square, encompass'd by two of our cavalry regiments, one of which regiments had three days before found the bloody corpses of three of their men hamstrung and hung up by the heels to limbs of trees by Moseby's guerillas, and the other had not long before had twelve men, after surrendering, shot and then hung by the neck to limbs of trees, and jeering inscriptions pinn'd to the breast of one of the corpses, who had been a sergeant. Those three, and those twelve, had been found, I say, by these environing regiments. Now, with revolvers, they form'd the grim cordon of their seventeen prisoners. The latter were placed in the midst of the hollow square, were unfasten'd, and the ironical remark made to them that they were now to be given "a chance for themselves." A few ran for it. But what use? From every side the deadly pills came. In a few minutes the seventeen corpses strew'd the hollow square. . . . . . . I was curious to know whether some of the Union soldiers, some few, (some one or two at least of the youngsters,) did not abstain from shooting on the helpless men. Not one. There was no exultation, very little said; almost nothing, yet every man there contributed his shot.

(Multiply the above by scores, aye hundreds — varify it in all the forms that different circumstances, individuals, places, &c., could afford — light it with every lurid passion, the wolf's, the lion's lapping thirst for blood, the passionate, boiling volcanoes of human revenge for comrades, brothers slain — with the light of burning farms, and heaps of smutting, smouldering black embers — and in the human heart everywhere black, worse embers — and you have an inkling of this War.)

Items Wanted — (From my Note Books.) — Some of the half-erased and not over-legible when made, memoranda of things wanted, by one patient or another, will convey quite a fair idea. D. S. G. bed 52, wants a good book; has a sore, weak throat; would like some horehound candy. Is from New Jersey, 28th regiment. . . . . . . C. H. L., 145th Pennsylvania, lies in bed 6, with jaundice and erysipelas; also wounded. Stomach easily nauseated. Bring him some oranges, also a little tart jelly. Hearty, full-blooded young fellow. (He got better in a few days, and is now home on a furlough.). . . . . . . J. H. G., bed 24, wants an undershirt, drawers and socks. Has not had a change for quite a while. Is evidently a neat clean boy from New England. I supplied him; also with a comb, tooth-brush, and some soap and towels. I noticed afterward he was the cleanest of the whole Ward. . . . . . . Mrs. G., lady nurse, Ward F., wants a bottle of brandy — has two patients imperatively requiring stimulus — low with wounds and exhaustion. (I supplied her with a bottle of first-rate brandy, from the Christian Commission rooms.)

Female Nurses for Soldiers. — There are many women in one position or another, among the Hospitals, mostly as nurses here in Washington, and among the military stations; quite a number of them young ladies acting as volunteers. They are a great help in certain ways, and deserve to be mention'd with praise and respect. Then it remains to be distinctly said that few or no young ladies, under the irresistible conventions of society, answer the practical requirements of nurses for soldiers. Middle-aged or healthy and good condition'd elderly women, mothers of children, are always best. Many of the wounded must be handled. A hundred things which cannot be gainsay'd, must occur and must be done. The presence of a good middle-aged or elderly woman, the magnetic touch of hands, the expressive features of the mother, the silent soothing of her presence, her words, her knowledge and privileges arrived at only through having had children, are precious and final qualifications. (Mrs. H. J. Wright, of Mansion House Hospital, Alexandria, is one of those good nurses. I have known her for over two years in her labors of love.) It is a natural faculty that is required; it is not merely having a genteel young woman at a table in a Ward. One of the finest nurses I met was a red-faced illiterate old Irish woman; I have seen her take the poor wasted naked boys so tenderly up in her arms. There are plenty of excellent clean old black women that would make tip-top nurses.

Wounds and Diseases. — The war is over, but the hospitals are fuller than ever, from former and current cases. A large majority of the wounds are in the arms and legs. But there is every kind of wound, in every part of the body. I should say of the sick, from my observation, that the prevailing maladies are typhoid fever and the camp fevers generally, diarrhœa, catarrhal affections and bronchitis, rheumatism and pneumonia. These forms of sickness lead; all the rest follow. There are twice as many sick as there are wounded. The deaths range from 7 to 10 per cent. of those under treatment.

Murder of President Lincoln. — The day, April 14, 1865, seems to have been a pleasant one throughout the whole land — the moral atmosphere pleasant too — the long storm, so dark, so fratricidal, full of blood and doubt and gloom, over and ended at last by the sun-rise of such an absolute National victory, and utter breaking-down of Secessionism — we almost doubted our own senses! Lee had capitulated beneath the apple-tree of Appomattax. The other armies, the flanges of the revolt, swiftly follow'd. . . . . . . And could it really be, then? Out of all the affairs of this world of woe and passion, of failure and disorder and dismay, was there really come the confirm'd, unerring sign of plan, like a shaft of pure light — of rightful rule — of God? . . . . So the day, as I say, was propitious. Early herbage, early flowers, were out. (I remember where I was stopping at the time, the season being advanced, there were many lilacs in full bloom. By one of those caprices that enter and give tinge to events without being at all a part of them, I find myself always reminded of the great tragedy of that day by the sight and odor of these blossoms. It never fails.)

But I must not dwell on accessories. The deed hastens. The popular afternoon paper of Washington, the little *Evening Star*, had spatter'd all over its third page, divided among the advertisements in a sensational manner in a hundred different places, *The President and his Lady will be at the Theatre this evening* . . . . (Lincoln was fond of the theatre. I have myself seen him there several times. I remember thinking how funny it was that He, in some respects, the leading actor in the greatest and stormiest drama known to real history's stage, through centuries, should sit there and be so completely interested and absorb'd in those human jack-straws, moving about with their silly little gestures, foreign spirit, and flatulent text.)

On this occasion the theatre was crowded, many ladies in rich and gay costumes, officers in their uniforms, many well known citizens, young folks, the usual clusters of gas-lights, the usual magnetism of so many people, cheerful, with perfumes, music of violins and flutes — (and over all, and saturating all, that vast vague wonder, *Victory*, the Nation's Victory, the triumph of the Union, filling the air, the thought, the sense, with exhilaration more than all perfumes.)

The President came betimes, and, with his wife, witness'd the play, from the large stage-boxes of the second tier, two thrown into one, and profusely draped with the National flag. The acts and scenes of the piece — one of those singularly written compositions which have at least the merit of giving entire relief to an audience engaged in mental action or business excitements and cares during the day, as it makes not the slightest call on either the moral, emotional, esthetic, or spiritual nature — a piece, ('Our American Cousin,') in which, among other characters, so call'd, a Yankee, certainly such a one as was never seen, or the least like it ever seen, in North America, is introduced in England, with a varied fol-de-rol of talk, plot, scenery, and such phantasmagoria as goes to make up a modern popular drama — had progress'd through perhaps a couple of its acts, when in the midst of this comedy, or tragedy, or non-such, or whatever it is to be call'd, and to off-set it or finish it out, as if in Nature's and the Great Muse's mockery of those poor mimes, comes interpolated that Scene, not really or exactly to be described at all, (for on the many hundreds who were there it seems to this hour to have left little but a passing blur, a dream, a blotch) — and yet partially to be described as I now proceed to give it. . . . . . There is a scene in the play representing a modern parlor, in which two unprecedented English ladies are inform'd by the unprecedented and impossible Yankee that he is not a man of fortune, and therefore undesirable for marriage-catching purposes; after which, the comments being finish'd, the dramatic trio make exit, leaving the stage clear for a moment. There was a pause, a hush as it were. At this period came the murder of Abraham Lincoln. Great as that was, with all its manifold train, circling round it, and stretching into the future for many a century, in the politics, history, art, &c., of the New World, in point of fact the main thing, the actual murder, transpired with the quiet and simplicity of any commonest occurrence — the bursting of a bud or pod in the growth of vegetation, for instance. Through the general hum following the stage pause, with the change of positions, &c., came the muffled sound of a pistol shot, which not one hundredth part of the audience heard at the time — and yet a moment's hush — somehow, surely a vague startled thrill — and then, through the ornamented, draperied, starr'd and striped space-way of the President's box, a sudden figure, a man raises himself with hands and feet, stands a moment on the railing, leaps below to the stage, (a distance of perhaps fourteen or fifteen feet,) falls out of position, catching his boot-heel in the copious drapery, (the American flag,) falls on one knee, quickly recovers himself, rises as if nothing had happen'd, (he really sprains his ankle, but unfelt then,) — and so the figure, Booth, the murderer, dress'd in plain black broadcloth, bare-headed, with a full head of glossy, raven hair, and his eyes like some mad animal's flashing with light and resolution, yet with a certain strange calmness, holds aloft in one hand a large knife — walks along not much back from the footlights — turns fully toward the audience his face of statuesque beauty, lit by those basilisk eyes, flashing with desperation, perhaps insanity — launches out in a firm and steady voice the words, *Sic semper tyrannis* — and then walks with neither slow nor very rapid pace diagonally across to the back of the stage, and disappears. . . . . . . (Had not all this terrible scene — making the mimic ones preposterous — had it not all been rehears'd, in blank, by Booth, beforehand?)

A moment's hush, incredulous — a scream — the cry of *Murder* — Mrs. Lincoln leaning out of the box, with ashy cheeks and lips, with involuntary cry, pointing to the retreating figure, *He has kill'd the President*. . . . . . . And still a moment's strange, incredulous suspense — and then the deluge! — then that mixture of horror, noises, uncertainty — (the sound, somewhere back, of a horse's hoofs clattering with speed) — the people burst through chairs and railings, and break them up — that noise adds to the queerness of the scene — there is inextricable confusion and terror — women faint — quite feeble persons fall, and are trampled on — many cries of agony are heard — the broad stage suddenly fills to suffocation with a dense and motley crowd, like some horrible carnival — the audience rush generally upon it — at least the strong men do — the actors and actresses are all there in their play-costumes and painted faces, with mortal fright showing through the rouge, some trembling — some in tears — the screams and calls, confused talk — redoubled, trebled — two or three manage to pass up water from the stage to the President's box — others try to clamber up — &c., &c., &c.

In the midst of all this, the soldiers of the President's Guard, with others, suddenly drawn to the scene, burst in — (some two hundred altogether) — they storm the house, through all the tiers, especially the upper ones, inflamed with fury, literally charging the audience with fix'd bayonets, muskets and pistols, shouting *Clear out! clear out! you sons of* — . . . . Such the wild scene, or a suggestion of it rather, inside the play-house that night.

Outside, too, in the atmosphere of shock and craze, crowds of people, fill'd with frenzy, ready to seize any outlet for it, come near committing murder several times on innocent individuals. One such case was especially exciting. The infuriated crowd, through some chance, got started against one man, either for words he utter'd, or perhaps without any cause at all, and were proceeding at once to actually hang him on a neighboring lamp post, when he was rescued by a few heroic policemen, who placed him in their midst and fought their way slowly and amid great peril toward the Station House. . . . . . . It was a fitting episode of the whole affair. The crowd rushing and eddying to and fro — the night, the yells, the pale faces, many frighten'd people trying in vain to extricate themselves — the attack'd man, not yet freed from the jaws of death, looking like a corpse — the silent resolute half-dozen policemen, with no weapons but their little clubs, yet stern and steady through all those eddying swarms — made indeed a fitting side-scene to the grand tragedy of the murder. . . . . . . They gain'd the Station House with the protected man, whom they placed in security for the night, and discharged him in the morning.

And in the midst of that night-pandemonium of senseless hate, infuri-ated soldiers, the audience and the crowd — the stage, and all its actors and actresses, its paint-pots, spangles, and gas-lights — the life-blood from those veins, the best and sweetest of the land, drips slowly down, and death's ooze already begins its little bubbles on the lips. . . . . . . Such, hurriedly sketch'd, were the accompaniments of the death of President Lincoln. So suddenly and in murder and horror unsurpass'd he was taken from us. But his death was painless.

[He leaves for America's History and Biography, so far, not only its most dramatic reminiscence — he leaves, in my opinion, the greatest, best, most characteristic, artistic, Personality. Not but that he had faults, and show'd them in the Presidency; but honesty, goodness, shrewdness, conscience, and (a new virtue, unknown to other lands, and hardly yet really known here, but the foundation and tie of all, as the future will grandly develop,) Unionism, in its truest and amplest sense, form'd the hard-pan of his character. These he seal'd with his life. The tragic splendor of his death, purging, illuminating all, throws round his form, his head, an aureole that will remain and will grow brighter through time, while History lives, and love of Country lasts. By many has *this Union* been conserv'd and help'd; but if one name, one man, must be pick'd out, he, most of all, is the Conservator of it, to the future. He was assassinated — but the Union is not assassinated — *ça ira!* One falls, and another falls. The soldier drops, sinks like a wave — but the ranks of the ocean eternally press on. Death does its work, obliterates a hundred, a thousand — President, general, captain, private — but the Nation is im-mortal.]

Releas'd Union Prisoners from South. — The releas'd prisoners of War are now coming up from the Southern prisons. I have seen a number of them. The sight is worse than any sight of battle-fields or any collections of wounded, even the bloodiest. There was, (as a sample,) one large boat load, of several hundreds, brought about the 25th, to Annapolis; and out of the whole number only three individ-uals were able to walk from the boat. The rest were carried ashore and laid down in one place or another. Can those be *men* — those little livid-brown, ash-streak'd, monkey-looking dwarfs? — are they really not mummied, dwindled corpses? They lay there, most of them, quite still, but with a horrible look in their eyes and skinny lips, often with not enough flesh on the lips to cover their teeth. Probably no more appalling sight was ever seen on this earth. (There are deeds, crimes, that may be forgiven; but this is not among them. It steeps its perpetra-tors in blackest, escapeless, endless damnation. Over 50,000 have been compell'd to die the death of starvation — reader, did you ever try to realize what *starvation* actually is? — in those prisons — and in a land of plenty!)

An indescribable meanness, tyranny, aggravating course of insults, almost incredible — was evidently the rule of treatment through all the Southern military prisons. The dead there are not to be pitied as much as some of the living that come from there — if they can be call'd living — many of them are mentally imbecile, and will never recuperate.

The Grand Review. — For two days now the broad spaces of Pennsylvania Avenue along to Treasury Hill, and so by detour around to the President's House, (and so up to Georgetown, and across the Aqueduct bridge,) have been alive with a magnificent sight, the returning Armies. In their wide ranks stretching clear across the Avenue I watch them march or ride along, at a brisk pace, through two whole days — Infantry, Cavalry, Artillery — some 200,000 men. . . . . Some days afterwards one or two other Corps . . . . and then, still afterwards, a good part of Sherman's immense Army, brought up from Charleston, Savannah, &c.

Two Brothers, one South, one North — May 28–9. — I staid to-night a long time by the bed-side of a new patient, a young Baltimorean, aged about 19 years, W. S. P., (2nd Md. Southern,) very feeble, right leg amputated, can't sleep hardly at all — has taken a great deal of morphine, which, as usual, is costing more than it comes to. Evidently very intelligent and well bred — very affectionate — held on to my hand, and put it by his face, not willing to let me leave. As I was lingering, soothing him in his pain, he says to me suddenly, "I hardly think you know who I am — I don't wish to impose upon you — I am a rebel soldier." I said I did not know that, but it made no difference. . . . . . . Visiting him daily for about two weeks after that, while he lived, (death had mark'd him, and he was quite alone,) I loved him much, always kiss'd him, and he did me.

In an adjoining Ward I found his brother, an officer of rank, a Union soldier, a brave and religious man, (Col. Clifton K. Prentiss, Sixth Md. Infantry, Sixth Corps, wounded in one of the engagements at Petersburgh, April 2 — linger'd, suffer'd much, died in Brooklyn, Aug. 20, '65.) It was in the same battle both were hit. One was a strong Unionist, the other Secesh; both fought on their respective sides, both badly wounded, and both brought together here after absence of four years. Each died for his cause.

Three Years Summ'd Up. — During my past three years in Hospital, camp or field, I made over 600 visits or tours, and went, as I estimate, among from 80,000 to 100,000 of the wounded and sick, as sustainer of spirit and body in some degree, in time of need. These visits varied from an hour or two, to all day or night; for with dear or critical cases I always watch'd all night. Sometimes I took up my quarters in the Hospital, and slept or watch'd there several nights in succession. Those three years I consider the greatest privilege and satisfaction, (with all their feverish excitements and physical deprivations and lamentable sights,) and, of course, the most profound lesson and reminiscence, of my life. I can say that in my ministerings I comprehended all, whoever came in my way, Northern or Southern, and slighted none. It afforded me, too, the perusal of those subtlest, rarest, divinest volumes of Humanity, laid bare in its inmost recesses, and of actual life and death, better than the finest, most labor'd narratives, histories, poems in the libraries. It arous'd and brought out and decided undream'd-of depths of emotion. It has given me my plainest and most fervent views of the true *ensemble* and extent of The States. While I was with wounded and sick in thousands of cases from the New England States, and from New York, New Jersey, and Pennsylvania, and from Michigan, Wisconsin, Ohio, Indiana, Illinois, and all the Western States, I was with more or less from all the States, North and South, without exception. I was with many from the Border States, especially from Maryland and Virginia, and found, during those lurid years 1862–65, far more Union Southerners, especially Tennesseans, than is supposed. I was with many rebel officers and men among our wounded, and gave them always what I had, and tried to cheer them the same as any. I was among the army teamsters considerably, and, indeed, always found myself drawn to them. Among the black soldiers, wounded or sick, and in the contraband camps, I also took my way whenever in their neighborhood, and did what I could for them.

The Million Dead, too, summ'd up — The Unknown. — The Dead in this War — there they lie, strewing the fields and woods and valleys and battle-fields of the South — Virginia, the Peninsula — Malvern Hill and Fair Oaks — the banks of the Chickahominy — the terraces of Fredericksburgh — Antietam bridge — the grisly ravines of Manassas — the bloody promenade of the Wilderness — the varieties of the *strayed* dead, (the estimate of the War Department is 25,000 National soldiers kill'd in battle and never buried at all, 5,000 drown'd — 15,000 inhumed by strangers or on the march in haste, in hitherto unfound localities — 2,000 graves cover'd by sand and mud, by Mississippi freshets, 3,000 carried away by caving-in of banks, &c.,) — Gettysburgh, the West, Southwest — Vicksburg — Chattanooga — the trenches of Petersburgh — the numberless battles, camps, Hospitals everywhere — the crop reap'd by the mighty reapers, Typhoid, Dysentery, Inflammations — and blackest and loathesomest of all, the dead and living burial-pits, the Prison-Pens of Andersonville, Salisbury, Belle-Isle, &c., (not Dante's pictured Hell and all its woes, its degradations, filthy torments, excell'd those Prisons) — the dead, the dead, the dead — *our* dead — or South or North, ours all, (all, all, all, finally dear to me) — or East or West — Atlantic Coast or Mississippi Valley — Some where they crawl'd to die, alone, in bushes, low gulleys, or on the sides of hills — (there, in secluded spots, their skeletons, bleach'd bones, tufts of hair, buttons, fragments of clothing, are occasionally found, yet) — our young men once so handsome and so joyous, taken from us — the son from the mother, the husband from the wife, the dear friend from the dear friend — the clusters of camp graves, in Georgia, the Carolinas, and in Tennessee — the single graves in the woods or by the road-side, (hundreds, thousands, obliterated) — the corpses floated down the rivers, and caught and lodged, (dozens, scores, floated down the Upper Potomac, after the cavalry engagements, the pursuit of Lee, following Gettysburgh) — some lie at the bottom of the sea — the general Million, and the special Cemeteries in almost all the States — the Infinite Dead — (the land entire is saturated, perfumed with their impalpable ashes' exhalation in Nature's chemistry distill'd, and shall be so forever, and every grain of wheat and ear of corn, and every flower that grows, and every breath we draw,) — not only Northern dead leavening Southern soil — thousands, aye many tens of thousands, of Southerners, crumble to-day in Northern earth.

And everywhere among these countless graves — everywhere in the many Soldiers Cemeteries of the Nation, (there are over seventy of them) — as at the time in the vast trenches, the depositaries of slain, Northern and Southern, after the great battles — not only where the scathing trail pass'd those years, but radiating since in all the peaceful quarters of the land — we see, and see, and ages yet may see, on monuments and gravestones, singly or in masses, to thousands or tens of thousands, the significant word

UNKNOWN.

(In some of the Cemeteries nearly *all* the dead are Unknown. At Salisbury, N. C., for instance, the known are only 85, while the Unknown are 12,027, and 11,700 of these are buried in trenches. A National Monument has been put up here, by order of Congress, to mark the spot — but what visible, material monument can ever fittingly commemorate that spot?)

As I write this conclusion — in the open air, latter part of June, 1875, a delicious forenoon, everything rich and fresh from last night's copious rain—ten years and more have pass'd away since that War, and its wholesale deaths, burials, graves. (*They* make indeed the true Memoranda of the War—mute, subtle, immortal.) From ten years' rain and snow, in their seasons—grass, clover, pine trees, orchards, forests—from all the noiseless miracles of soil and sun and running streams—how peaceful and how beautiful appear to-day even the Battle-Trenches, and the many hundred thousand Cemetery mounds! Even at Andersonville, to-day, innocence and a smile. (A late account says, 'The stockade has fallen to decay, is grown upon, and a season more will efface it entirely, except from our hearts and memories. The *dead line*, over which so many brave soldiers pass'd to the freedom of eternity rather than endure the misery of life, can only be traced here and there, for most of the old marks the last ten years have obliterated. The thirty-five wells, which the prisoners dug with cups and spoons, remain just as they were left. And the wonderful spring which was discover'd one morning, after a thunder storm, flowing down the hillside, still yields its sweet, pure water as freely now as then. The Cemetery, with its thirteen thousand graves, is on the slope of a beautiful hill. Over the quiet spot already trees give the cool shade which would have been so gratefully sought by the poor fellows whose lives were ended under the scorching sun.')

And now, to thought of these—on these graves of the dead of the War, as on an altar—to memory of these, or North or South, I close and dedicate my book.

SELECTED LETTERS

Mrs. Louisa Whitman, Brooklyn

Washington,
Monday forenoon, Dec. 29, 1862.

Dear, Dear Mother — Friday the 19th inst. I succeeded in reaching the camp of the 51st New York, and found George alive and well.[1] In order to make sure that you would get the good news, I sent back by messenger to Washington a telegraphic dispatch (I dare say you did not get it for some time) as well as a letter — and the same to Hannah at Burlington. I have staid in camp with George ever since, till yesterday, when I came back to Washington, about the 24th. George got Jeff's[2] letter of the 20th. Mother, how much you must have suffered, all that week, till George's letter came — and all the rest must too. As to me, I know I put in about three days of the greatest suffering I ever experienced in my life. I wrote to Jeff how I had my pocket picked in a jam and hurry, changing cars, at Philadelphia — so that I landed here without a dime. The next two days I spent hunting through the hospitals, walking day and night, unable to ride, trying to get information — trying to get access to big people, etc. — I could not get the least clue to anything. Odell would not see me at all. But Thursday afternoon, I lit on a way to get down on the Government boat that runs to Aquia creek, and so by railroad to the neighborhood of Falmouth, opposite Fredericksburg — so by degrees I worked my way to Ferrero's brigade, which I found Friday afternoon without much trouble after I got in camp. When I found dear brother George, and found that he was alive and well, O you may imagine how trifling all my little cares and difficulties seemed — they vanished into nothing. And now that I have lived for eight or nine days amid such scenes as the camps furnish, and had a practical part in it all, and realize the way that hundreds of thousands of good men are now living, and have had to live for a year or more, not only without any of the comforts, but with death and sickness and hard marching and hard fighting (and no success at that) for their

---

1. *George ... well*] Whitman's brother George, who was ten years younger, had enlisted in the 51st New York Volunteers. He was reported wounded at the battle of Fredericksburg, Virginia, in December 1862. Whitman left Brooklyn for the front on December 16.

2. *Jeff's*] Thomas Jefferson Whitman, another brother.

continual experience — really nothing we call trouble seems worth talking about. One of the first things that met my eyes in camp was a heap of feet, arms, legs, etc., under a tree in front of a hospital, the Lacy house.

George is very well in health, has a good appetite — I think he is at times more wearied out and homesick than he shows, but stands it upon the whole very well. Every one of the soldiers, to a man, wants to get home.

I suppose Jeff got quite a long letter I wrote, from camp, about a week ago. I told you that George had been promoted to captain — his commission arrived while I was there. When you write, address, Capt. George W. Whitman, Co. K., 51st New York Volunteers, Ferrero's brigade, near Falmouth, Va. Jeff must write oftener, and put in a few lines from mother, even if it is only two lines — then in the next letter a few lines from Mat, and so on. You have no idea how letters from home cheer one up in camp, and dissipate homesickness.

While I was there George still lived in Capt. Francis's tent — there were five of us altogether, to eat, sleep, write, etc., in a space twelve feet square, but we got along very well — the weather all along was very fine — and would have got along to perfection, but Capt. Francis is not a man I could like much — I had very little to say to him. George is about building a place, half hut and half tent, for himself, (he is probably about it this very day,) and then he will be better off, I think. Every captain has a tent, in which he lives, transacts company business, etc., has a cook, (or a man of all work,) and in the same tent mess and sleep his lieutenants, and perhaps the first sergeant. They have a kind of fireplace — and the cook's fire is outside on the open ground. George had very good times while Francis was away — the cook, a young disabled soldier, Tom, is an excellent fellow and a first-rate cook, and the second lieutenant, Pooley, is a tip-top young Pennsylvanian. Tom thinks all the world of George; when he heard he was wounded, on the day of the battle, he left everything, got across the river, and went hunting for George through the field, through thick and thin. I wrote to Jeff that George was wounded by a shell, a gash in the cheek — you could stick a splint through into the mouth, but it has healed up without difficulty already. Everything is uncertain about the army, whether it moves or stays where it is. There are no furloughs granted at present. I will stay here for the present, at any rate long enough to see if I can get any employment at anything, and shall write what luck I have. Of course I am unsettled at present. Dear mother, my love.

Walt.

If Jeff or any writes, address me, care of Major Hapgood, paymaster, U.S.A. Army, Washington, D.C. I send my love to dear sister Mat, and little Sis — and to Andrew and all my brothers.[3] O Mat, how lucky it was you did not come — together, we could never have got down to see George.

Nat Bloom and Fred Gray, New York

Washington, March 19, 1863.

Dear Nat and Fred Gray:

Since I left New York I was down in the Army of the Potomac in front with my brother a good part of the winter, commencing time of the battle of Fredericksburgh — have seen *war-life*, the real article — folded myself in a blanket, lying down in the mud with composure — relished salt pork and hard tack — have been on the battlefield among the wounded, the faint and the bleeding, to give them nourishment — have gone over with a flag of truce the next day to help direct the burial of the dead — have struck up a tremendous friendship with a young Mississippi captain (about 19) that we took prisoner badly wounded at Fredericksburgh (he has followed me here, is in the Emory hospital here minus a leg — he wears his confederate uniform, proud as the devil — I met him first at Falmouth, in the Lacy house middle of December last, his leg just cut off, and cheered him up — poor boy, he has suffered a great deal, and still suffers — has eyes bright as a hawk, but face pale — our affection is an affair quite romantic — sometimes when I lean over to say I am going, he puts his arms around my neck, draws my face down, etc., quite a scene for the New Bowery). I spent the Christmas holidays on the Rappahannock. — During January came up hither, took a lodging room here. Did the 37th Congress, especially the night sessions the last three weeks, explored the Capitol, meandering the gorgeous painted interminable Senate corridors, getting lost in them (a new sensation, rich and strong, that endless painted interior at night) — got very much interested in some particular cases in Hospitals here — go now steadily to more or less of said Hospitals by day or night — find always the sick and dying soldiers forthwith begin to cling to me in a way that makes a fellow feel funny enough. These Hospitals, so different from all others — these thousands, and tens and twenties of thousands of

---

3. *Mat . . . brothers*] Jeff Whitman's wife Martha (Mat), their daughter Mannahatta (little Sis) and another brother, Andrew Jackson Whitman. Walt Whitman was one of nine children.

American young men, badly wounded, all sorts of wounds, operated on, pallid with diarrhœa, languishing, dying with fever, pneumonia, etc., open a new world somehow to me, giving closer insights, new things, exploring deeper mines, than any yet, showing our humanity (I sometimes put myself in fancy in the cot, with typhoid, or under the knife) tried by terrible, fearfullest tests, probed deepest, the living soul's, the body's tragedies, bursting the petty bonds of art. To these, what are your dramas and poems, even the oldest and the fearfullest? Not old Greek mighty ones; where man contends with fate (and always yields) — not Virgil showing Dante on and on among the agonized and damned, approach what here I see and take part in. For here I see, not at intervals, but quite always, how certain man, our American man — how he holds himself cool and unquestioned master above all pains and bloody mutilations. It is immense, the best thing of all — nourishes me of all men. This then, what frightened us all so long. Why, it is put to flight with ignominy — a mere stuffed scarecrow of the fields. Oh death, where is thy sting? Oh grave, where is thy victory?

In the Patent Office, as I stood there one night, just off the cot-side of a dying soldier, in a large ward that had received the worst cases of Second Bull Run, Antietam, and Fredericksburgh, the surgeon, Dr. Stone (Horatio Stone the Sculptor) told me, of all who had died in that crowded ward the past six months, he had still to find the *first man* or *boy* who had met the approach of death with a single tremor or unmanly fear. But let me change the subject — I have given you screed enough about Death and the Hospitals — and too much — since I got started. Only I have some curious yarns I promise you my darlings and gossips, by word of mouth whene'er we meet.

Washington and its points I find bear a second and a third perusal, and doubtless many. My first impressions, architectural, etc., were not favorable; but upon the whole, the city, the spaces, buildings, etc., make no unfit emblem of our country, so far, so broadly planned, everything in plenty, money and materials staggering with plenty, but the fruit of the plans, the knit, the combination yet wanting — Determined to express ourselves greatly in a Capitol but no fit Capitol yet here (time, associations, wanting I suppose) many a hiatus yet — many a thing to be taken down and done over again yet — perhaps an entire change of base — maybe a succession of changes.

Congress does not seize very hard upon me; I studied it and its members with curiosity, and long — much gab, great fear of public opinion, plenty of low business talent, but no masterful man in Congress (probably best so). I think well of the President. He has a face like a Hoosier Michael Angelo, so awful ugly it becomes beautiful, with its strange mouth, its deep cut, criss-cross lines, and its doughnut complexion. — My notion is too, that underneath his outside smutched mannerism, and stories from third-class county barrooms (it is his humor), Mr. Lincoln keeps a fountain of first-class practical telling wisdom. I do not dwell on the supposed failures of his government; he has shown, I sometimes think an almost supernatural tact in keeping the ship afloat at all, with head steady, not only not going down, and now certain not to, but with proud and resolute spirit, and flag flying in sight of the world, menacing and high as ever. I say never yet captain, never ruler, had such a perplexing dangerous task as his, the past two years. I more and more rely upon his idiomatic western genius, careless of court dress or court decorum.

I am living here without much definite aim (except going to the hospitals) — yet I have quite a good time — I make some money by scribbling for the papers, and as copyist. I have had (and have) thoughts of trying to get a clerkship or something, but I only try in a listless sort of way, and of course do not succeed. I have strong letters of introduction from Mr. Emerson to Mr. Seward and Mr. Chase, but I have not presented them. I have seen Mr. Sumner several times anent my office hunting — he promised fair once — but he does not seem to be finally fascinated. I hire a bright little 3rd story front room, with service, etc., for $7 a month, dine in the same house (394 L St. a private house) — and remain yet much of the old vagabond that so gracefully becomes me. I miss you all, my darlings and gossips, Fred Gray, and Bloom and Russell and everybody. I wish you would all come here in a body — that would be divine (we would drink ale, which is here the best). My health, strength, personal beauty, etc., are, I am happy to inform you, without diminution, but on the contrary quite the reverse. I weigh full 220 pounds avoirdupois, yet still retain my usual perfect shape — a regular model. My beard, neck, etc., are woolier, fleecier, whiteyer than ever. I wear army boots, with magnificent black morocco tops, the trousers put in, wherein shod and legged, confront I Virginia's deepest mud with supercilious eyes. The scenery around Washington is really fine, the Potomac a lordly river, the hills, woods, etc., all attractive. I poke about quite a good deal. Much of the weather here is from heaven — of late though, a stretch decidedly from the other point. To-night (for it is night about 10) I sit alone writing this epistle (which will doubtless devour you all with envy and admiration) in a room adjoining my own particular. A gentleman and his wife who occupy the two other apartments on this floor have gone to see Heron in *Medea* — have put their little child in bed and left me in charge. The little one is sleeping soundly there in the back room, and I (plagued with a cold in the head) sit here in the front by a good fire writing as aforesaid to my gossips and darlings. The evening is lonesome and still, I am entirely alone "Oh, Solitude where are the charms, etc."

Now you write to me good long letters, my own boys. You, Bloom, give me your address particular, dear friend. Tell me Charles Russell's address, particular — also write me about Charles Chauncey. Tell me about everybody. For, dearest gossips, as the heart panteth, etc., so my soul after any and all sorts of items about you all. My darling, dearest boys, if I could be with you this hour, long enough to take only just three mild hot rums, before cool weather closes.

Friday Morning, 20th — I finish my letter in the office of Major Hapgood, a paymaster, and a friend of mine. This is a large building filled with paymaster's offices, some thirty or forty or more. This room is up on the fifth floor (a most noble and broad view from my window) curious scenes around here — a continual stream of soldiers, officers, cripples, etc., some climbing wearily up the stairs. They seek their pay — and every hour, almost every minute, has its incident, its hitch, its romance, farce or tragedy. There are two paymasters in this room. A sentry at the street door, another halfway up the stairs, another at the chief clerk's door, all with muskets and bayonets — sometimes a great swarm, hundreds around the side walk in front waiting (everybody is waiting for something here). I take a pause, look up a couple of minutes from my pen and paper — see spread, off there the Potomac, very fine, nothing petty about it — the Washington monument, not half finished — the public grounds around it filled with ten thousand beeves on the hoof — to the left the Smithsonian with its brown turrets — to the right far across, Arlington Heights, the forts, eight or ten of them — then the long bridge, and down a ways but quite plain, the shipping of Alexandria. Opposite me, and in a stone throw is the Treasury Building, and below the bustle and life of Pennsylvania Avenue. I shall hasten with my letter, and then go forth and take a stroll down "the avenue" as they call it here.

Now you boys, don't you think I have done the handsome thing by writing this astoundingly magnificent letter — certainly the longest I ever wrote in my life. Fred, I wish you to present my best respects to your father, Bloom and all; one of these days we will meet, and make up for lost time, my dearest boys.

Walt.

Address me, care Major Hapgood, paymaster U.S. Army, Cor. 15th & F St., Washington. How is Mullen? Give him my respects — How is Ben Knower? How the twinkling and temperate Towle? Remember me to them.

Mrs. Louisa Whitman, Brooklyn

Washington, June 30th, 1863.

Dearest Mother — Your letter, with Han's,[4] I have sent to George, though whether it will find him or not I cannot tell, as I think the 51st must be away down at Vicksburg. I have not had a word from George yet. Mother, I have had quite an attack of sore throat and distress in my head for some days past, up to last night, but to-day I feel nearly all right again. I have been about the city same as usual nearly — to the hospitals, etc., I mean. I am told that I hover too much over the beds of the hospitals, with fever and putrid wounds, etc. One soldier brought here about fifteen days ago, very low with typhoid fever, Livingston Brooks, Co. B., 17th Penn. Cavalry, I have particularly stuck to, as I found him to be in what appeared to be a dying condition, from negligence and a horrible journey of about forty miles, bad roads and fast driving; and then after he got here, as he is a simple country boy, very shy and silent, and made no complaint, they neglected him. I found him something like I found John Holmes last winter. I called the doctor's attention to him, shook up the nurses, had him bathed in spirits, gave him lumps of ice, and ice to his head; he had a fearful bursting pain in his head, and his body was like fire. He was very quiet, a very sensible boy, old fashioned; he did not want to die, and I had to lie to him without stint, for he thought I knew everything, and I always put in of course that what I told him was exactly the truth, and that if he got really dangerous I would tell him and not conceal it. The rule is to remove bad fever patients out from the main wards to a tent by themselves, and the doctor told me he would have to be removed. I broke it gently to him, but the poor boy got it immediately in his head that he was marked with death, and was to be removed on that account. It had a great effect upon him, and although I told the truth this time it did not have as good a result as my former fibs. I persuaded the doctor to let him remain. For three days he lay just about an even chance, go or stay, with a little leaning toward the first. But, mother, to make a long story short, he is now out of any immediate danger. He has been perfectly rational throughout — begins to taste a little food (for a week he ate nothing; I had to compel him to take a quarter of an orange now and then), and I will say, whether anyone calls it pride or not, that if he *does* get up and around again it's me that saved his life. Mother, as I have said in former letters, you can have no idea how these sick and dying youngsters cling to a fellow, and how fascinating it is, with all its hospital surroundings of sadness and scenes of repulsion and death. In this same hospital, Armory-square, where this

4. *Han's*] Whitman's sister, Hannah Heyde.

cavalry boy is, I have about fifteen or twenty particular cases I see much to — some of them as much as him. There are two from East Brooklyn: George Monk, Co. A, 78th N.Y., and Stephen Redgate (his mother is a widow in East Brooklyn — I have written to her). Both are pretty badly wounded — both are youngsters under 19. O mother, it seems to me as I go through these rows of cots as if it was too bad to accept these *children*, to subject them to such premature experiences. I devote myself much to Armory-square hospital because it contains by far the worst cases, most repulsive wounds, has the most suffering and most need of consolation. I go every day without fail, and often at night — sometimes stay very late. No one interferes with me, guards, nurses, doctors, nor anyone. I am let to take my own course.

Well, mother, I suppose you folks think we are in a somewhat dubious position here in Washington, with Lee in strong force almost between us and you Northerners. Well, it does look ticklish; if the Rebs cut the connection then there will be fun. The Reb cavalry come quite near us, dash in and steal wagon trains, etc.; it would be funny if they should come some night to the President's country house (Soldier's home), where he goes out to sleep every night; it is in the same direction as their saucy raid last Sunday. Mr. Lincoln passes here (14th st.) every evening on his way out. I noticed him last evening about half-past 6 — he was in his barouche, two horses, guarded by about thirty cavalry. The barouche comes first under a slow trot, driven by one man in the box, no servant or footmen beside; the cavalry all follow closely after with a lieutenant at their head. I had a good view of the President last evening. He looks more careworn even than usual, his face with deep cut lines, seams, and his *complexion gray* through very dark skin — a curious looking man, very sad. I said to a lady who was looking with me, "Who can see that man without losing all wish to be sharp upon him personally?" The lady assented, although she is almost vindictive on the course of the administration (thinks it wants nerve, etc. — the usual complaint). The equipage is rather shabby, horses indeed almost what my friends the Broadway drivers would call *old plugs*. The President dresses in plain black clothes, cylinder hat — he was alone yesterday. As he came up, he first drove over to the house of the Sec. of War, on K st., about 300 feet from here; sat in his carriage while Stanton came out and had a 15 minutes interview with him (I can see from my window), and then wheeled around the corner and up Fourteenth st., the cavalry after him. I really think it would be safer for him just now to stop at the White House, but I expect he is too proud to abandon the former custom. Then about an hour after we had a large cavalry regiment pass, with blankets, arms, etc., on the war march over the same track. The regt. was very full, over a thousand—indeed thirteen or fourteen hundred. It was an old regt., veterans, *old fighters*, young as they were. They were preceeded by a fine mounted band of sixteen (about ten bugles, the rest cymbals and drums). I tell you, mother, it made everything ring—made my heart leap. They played with a will. Then the accompaniment: the sabers rattled on a thousand men's sides—they had pistols, their heels were spurred—handsome American young men (I make no acc't of any other); rude uniforms, well worn, but good cattle, prancing—all good riders, full of the devil; nobody shaved, very sunburnt. The regimental officers (splendidly mounted, but just as roughly dressed as the men) came immediately after the band, then company after company, with each its officers at its head—the tramps of so many horses (there is a good hard turnpike)—then a long train of men with led horses, mounted negroes, and a long, long string of baggage wagons, each with four horses, and then a strong rear guard. I tell you it had the look of *real war*—noble looking fellows; a man feels so proud on a good horse, and armed. They are off toward the region of Lee's (supposed) rendezvous, toward Susquehannah, for the great anticipated battle. Alas! how many of these healthy, handsome, rollicking young men will lie cold in death before the apples ripen in the orchard. Mother, it is curious and stirring here in some respects. Smaller or larger bodies of troops are moving continually—many just-well men are turned out of the hospitals. I am where I see a good deal of them. There are getting to be *many black troops*. There is one very good regt. here black as tar; they go around, have the regular uniform—they submit to no nonsense. Others are constantly forming. It is getting to be a common sight. . . .[5]

Hugo Fritsch, New York

[Oct. 8, '63.]

Dear Hugo. I don't know why I have delayed so long as a month to write to you, for your affectionate and lively letter of September 5th gave me as much pleasure as I ever received from correspondence. I read it even yet & have taken the liberty to show it to one or two persons I knew would be interested. Dear comrade, you must be assured that my heart is much with you in New York, & with my other dear friends, your associates—& my dear I wish you to excuse me to Fred Gray & to Perk, & Ben Knower, for not yet writing to them, also to Charles Kingsley,

---

5. *sight. . . .*] The rest of this letter is missing.

should you see him — I am contemplating a tremendous letter to my dear comrade Frederickus, which will make up for deficiencies, — my own comrade Fred, how I should like to see him and have a good heart's time with him, & a mild orgie, just for a basis, you know, for talk & interchange of reminiscences & the play of the quiet lambent electricity of real friendship — O Hugo, as my pen glides along writing these thoughts, I feel as if I could not delay coming right off to New York & seeing you all, you & Fred & Bloom, & everybody — I want to see you, to be within hand's reach of you, and hear your voices, even if only for one evening for only three hours — I want to hear Perk's fiddle — I want to hear Perk himself, (& I will humbly submit to drink to the Church of England) — I want to be with Bloom (that wretched young man who I hear continually adorns himself outwardly, but I hear nothing of the interior) and I want to see Charley Russell, & if he is in N.Y. you see him I wish you to say that I sent him my love, particular, & that he & Fred & Charles Chauncey remain a group of itself in the portrait-gallery of my heart and mind yet & forever — for so it happened for our dear times, when we first got acquainted, (we recked not of them as they passed,) were so good, so hearty, those friendship times, our talk, our knitting together, it may be a whim, but I think nothing could be better or quieter & more happy of the kind — & is there any better kind in life's experiences? —

Dear comrade, I still live here as a hospital missionary after my own style, & on my own hook — I go every day or night without fail to some of the great government hospitals — O the sad scenes I witness — scenes of death, anguish, the fevers, amputations, friendlessness, hungering & thirsting young hearts, for some loving presence — such noble young men as some of these wounded are — such endurance, such native decorum, such candor — I will confess to you dear Hugo that in some respects I find myself in my element amid these scenes — shall I not say to you that I find I supply often to some of these dear suffering boys in my presence & magnetism that which nor doctors, nor medicines, nor skill, nor any routine assistance can give? Dear Hugo, you must write to me often as you can, & not delay it, your letters are very dear to me. Did you see my newspaper letter in N Y *Times* of Sunday Oct 4? About my dear comrade Bloom, is he still out in Pleasant Valley? Does he meet you often? Do you & the fellows meet at Gray's or anywhere? O Hugo I wish I could hear with you the current opera — I saw Devereux in the N Y papers of Monday announced for that night, & I knew in all probability you would be there — tell me how it goes, & about the principal singers — only don't run away with that theme, & occupy too much of your letter with it — but tell me mainly about all my dear friends, & every little personal item, & what you all do, & say &c.

I am excellent well. I have cut my beard short & hair ditto: (all my acquaintances are in anger & despair & go about wringing their hands) my face is all tanned & red. If the weather is moist or has been lately, or looks as if it thought of going to be, I perambulate this land in big army boots outside & up to my knees. Then around my majestic brow around my well-brimmed felt hat — a black & gold cord with acorns. Altogether the effect is satisfactory. The guards as I enter or pass places often salute me. All of which I tell, as you will of course take pride in your friend's special & expanding glory.

Fritschy, I am writing this in Major Hapgood's office, fifth story, by a window that overlooks all down the city, & over & down the beautiful Potomac, & far across the hills & shores for many a mile. We have had superb weather lately, yes for a month — it has just rained, so the dust is provided for, (that is the only thing I dread in Washington, the dust, I don't mind the mud). It is now between one and two o'clock Thursday afternoon. I am much alone in this pleasant far-up room, as Major is absent sick, & the clerk lays off a good deal. From three to five hours a day or night I go regularly among the sick, wounded, dying young men. I am enabled to give them things, food. There are very few visitors, amateurs, now. It has become an old story. The suffering ones cling to me poor children very close. I think of coming to New York quite soon to stay perhaps three weeks, then sure return here.

Julia Elizabeth Stilwell [South Norwalk, Connecticut][6]

[Oct. 21, '63.]

Dear friend, Jimmy is getting along favorably but of course slowly. I was with him night before last and am going again this afternoon. It requires a good deal of patience in him to lay so steadily confined in bed, but he has the good luck to continue remarkably free from any acute suffering so far. Night before last he had some pain and swelling in the foot below the wound, but nothing of serious account. They bandaged it pretty tightly and that relieved it. He wished me to write to *you* this time, and I promised him to do so night before last. I wrote at that time from the hospital to your parents at Comac, and sent the letter yesterday. Jim is not satisfied unless I write pretty often, whether there is anything to tell or not.

My friend I received your note about your folks getting your dear

---

6. *Julia . . . Connecticut*] A typical letter written for a wounded soldier.

brother's body from down in Virginia. Lately, as you doubtless know, the Rebels have advanced upon us, and have held Culpepper and around there for many days past; and of course nothing could be done. The rumor just now is that they are falling back, and may soon yield us our old ground. At present still I should think nothing could be done. The authorities here don't grant passes yet. But I suppose you inferred all this from what you read in the papers.

Dear friends all I say to you as I have to Jimmy's parents, that I shall try to keep watch of the boy, as according to all I know at present I shall probably continue in Washington for some time, and if any thing should occur I will write you. Dear friends, as it may be some reliance to you and make you feel less uneasy to know Jim can have nothing happen to him without you being informed. Though as far as now appears he will go on favorably, and his wound will heal up, so that he can sit up, and then gradually move about, and then in due time be able to travel.

So farewell for [the] present, and I pray that God may be with you, and though we are strangers I send my love to you and Jimmy's sisters and brothers in law, for in times of trouble and death, I see we draw near in spirit, regardless of being separated by distance, or of being unknown.

Lewis Kirk Brown and Hospital Comrades, Washington

Brooklyn, November 8, 1863.

Dear son and comrade, and all my dear comrades in the hospital I sit down this pleasant Sunday forenoon intending to write you all a good stout letter to try to amuse you as I am not able at present to visit you like I did — yet what I shall write about I hardly know until I get started — but my dear comrades I wish to help you pass away the time for a few minutes anyhow — I am now home at my mother's in Brooklyn N. Y. — I am in good health as ever and eat my rations without missing one time — Lew I wish you was here with me, and I wish my dear comrade Elijah Fox in ward G was here with me — but perhaps he is on his way to Wisconsin — Lewy I came through from Washington to New York by day train, 2nd Nov. had a very pleasant trip, everything went lovely, and I got home in the evening between 8 and 9 — Next morning I went up to the polls bright and early — I suppose it is not necessary to tell you how I voted — we have gained a great victory in this city — it went union this time, though it went democratic strong only a year ago, and for many years past — and all through the State the election was a very big thing for the union — I tell you the copperheads got flaxed out handsomely —

indeed these late elections are about as great a victory for us as if we had flaxed General Lee himself, and all his men — and so for personal good will I feel as if I could have more for Lee or any of his fighting men, than I have for the northern copperheads — Lewy I was very glad to get your letter of the 5th — I want you to tell Oscar Cunningham in your ward that I sent him my love and he must try to keep up good courage while he is confined there with his wound. Lewy I want you to give my love to Charley Cate and all the boys in ward K, and to Benton if he is there still — I wish you would go in ward C and see James O. Stilwell, and also Thomas Carson in same ward, and Chambers that lays next to him, and tell them I sent them my love. Give Carson this letter to read if he wishes it. Tell James Stilwell I have writ from here to his folks in Comac L I, and it may be I shall go down there next week on the L I railroad; and let him have this letter to read if he wishes it. Tell Manvill Winterstein that lays next to him in ward C that I send him my love, and I hope his wound is healing good. Lew I wish you to go in ward B and tell a young cavalry man, his first name is Edwin, he is wounded in the right arm, that I send him my love, and on the opposite side a young man wounded in the right knee, and also a young man named Charley wounded in left hand, and Jennings and also a young man I love that lays now up by the door just above Jennings, that I sent them all my love. So Lew you see I am giving you a good round job, with so many messages — but I want you to do them all dear son, and leave my letter with each of the boys that wish it, to read for themselves — tell Miss Gregg in ward A that I send my love to Pleasant Barley, if he is still there, and if so I hope it will be God's will that he will live and get strong to go home yet — I send my love to little Billy the Ohio boy in ward A, and to Miss Gregg herself — and if Miss Doolittle is in ward B, please ask her to tell the boys in the ward I sent them my love, and to her too, and give her this letter some evening to read to the boys, and one of these days I will come back and read to them myself — and the same to Mrs. Southwick in ward H, if she wishes to read it to the boys for my sake. Lew I wish you would go in ward G and find a very dear friend of mine in bed 11, Elijah D. Fox if he is still there. Tell him I sent him my best love and that I made reckoning of meeting him again, and that he must not forget me, though that I know he never will — I want to hear how he is, and whether he has got his papers through yet — Lewy I wish you would go to him first and let him have this letter to read if he is there — Lewy I would like you to give my love to a young man named Burns in ward I, and to all the boys in ward I. — and indeed in every ward, from A to K inclusive, and all through the hospital, as I find I cannot particularize without being tedious — so I send my love sincerely to each and all, for every sick and wounded soldier is dear to me as a son or brother, and furthermore every man that wears the union uniform and sticks to it like a man, is to me a dear comrade, and I will do what I can for him though it may not be much — and I will add that my mother and all my folks feel just the same about it, and would show it by their words too when they can ——

Well, dear comrades, what shall I tell you to pass away the time? I am going around quite a good deal, more than I really desire to. Two or three nights ago I went to the N Y Academy of Music, to the Italian opera. I suppose you know that is a performance, a play, all in music and singing, in the Italian language, very sweet and beautiful. There is a large company of singers and a large band, altogether two or three hundred. It is a splendid great house, four or five tiers high, and a broad parquette on the main floor. The opera here now has some of the greatest singers in the world — the principal lady singer (her name is Medori) has a voice that would make you hold your breath with wonder and delight — it is like a miracle — no mocking bird or clearest flute can begin with it — and besides she is a tall and handsome lady, and her actions are so graceful as she moves about the stage, playing her part. Boys, I must tell you just one scene in the opera I saw — things have worked so in the piece that this lady is compelled, although she tries very hard to avoid it, to give the cup of poisoned wine to her lover — the king her husband forces her to do it — she pleads hard, but her husband threatens to take both their lives (all this is in the singing and music, very fine) — so the lover is brought in as a prisoner, and the king pretends to pardon him and make up, and asks the young man to drink a cup of wine, and orders the lady to pour it out. The lover drinks it, then the king gives her and him a look, and walks off the stage. And now came as good a piece of performance as I ever saw in my life. The lady as soon as she saw that her husband was really gone, she sprang to her lover, clutched him by the arm, and poured out the greatest singing you ever heard — it poured like a raging river more than anything else I could compare it to — she tells him he is poisoned — he tries to inquire &c and hardly knows what to make of it — she breaks in trying to pacify him, and explain &c — all this goes on very rapid indeed, and the band accompanying — she quickly draws out from her bosom a little vial, to neutralize the poison, then the young man in his desperation abuses her and tells her perhaps it is to poison him still more as she has already poisoned him once — this puts her in such agony, she begs and pleads with him to take the antidote at once before it is too late — her voice is so wild and high it goes through one like a knife, yet it is delicious — she holds the little vial to his mouth with one hand and with the other springs open a secret door in the wall for him to escape from the palace — he swallows the antidote, and as she pushes him through the door, the husband returns with some armed guards, but she slams the door to, and stands back up against the door, and her arms spread wide open across it, one fist clenched, and her eyes glaring like a wildcat, so they dare not touch her — and that ends the scene. Comrades, recollect all this is in singing and music, and lots of it too, on a big scale, in the band, every instrument you can think of, and the best players in the world, and sometimes the whole band and the whole men's chorus and the women's chorus all putting on the steam together — and all in a vast house, light as day, and with a crowded audience of ladies and men. Such singing and strong rich music always give me the greatest pleasure — and so the opera is the only amusement I have gone to, for my own satisfaction, for last ten years.

But my dear comrades I will now tell you something about my own folks — home here there is quite a lot of us — my father is not living — my dear mother is very well indeed for her age, which is 67 — she is cheerful and hearty and still does all her light housework and cooking — She never tires of hearing about the soldiers, and I sometimes think she is the greatest patriot I ever met, one of the old stock — I believe she would cheerfully give her life for the union, if it would avail anything — and the last mouthful in the house to any union soldier that needed it — then I have a very excellent sister-in-law, — she has two fine young ones — so I am very happy in the women and family arrangements. Lewy, the brother I mentioned as sick, lives near here, he is very poorly indeed, and I fear will never be much better — he too was a soldier, has for several months had throat disease — he is married and has a family — I believe I have told you of still another brother in the army, down in the 9th Army Corps, has been in the service over two years, he is very rugged and healthy — has been in many battles, but only once wounded, at first Fredericksburg.

Elijah [Douglass] Fox

Brooklyn Saturday night Nov 21, '63.

Dear son and comrade. I wrote a few lines about five days ago and sent on to Armory Square, but as I have not heard from it I suppose you have gone on to Michigan. I got your letter of Nov. 10th and it gave me much comfort. Douglass I shall return to Washington about the 24th so when you write direct to care of Major Hapgood, paymaster U S A, Washington D C — Dearest comrade I only write this lest the one I wrote five days ago may not reach you from the hospital. I am still here at my

mother's and feel as if I have had enough of going around New York —
enough of amusements, suppers, drinking, and what is called
pleasure. — Dearest son: it would be more pleasure if we could be
together just in quiet, in some plain way of living, with some good
employment and reasonable income, where I could have you often with
me, than all the dissipations and amusements of this great city — O I
hope things may work so that we can yet have each other's society — for I
cannot bear the thought of being separated from you — I know I am a
great fool about such things but I tell you the truth dear son. I do not
think one night has passed in New York or Brooklyn when I have been at
the theatre or opera or afterward to some supper party or carousal made
by the young fellows for me, but what amid the play or the singing I
would perhaps think of you, — and the same at the gayest supper party of
men where all was fun and noise and laughing and drinking, of a dozen
young men and I among them I would see your face before me in my
thought as I have seen it so often there in Ward G, and my amusement
or drink would be all turned to nothing, and I would realize how happy
it would be if I could leave all the fun and noise and the crowd and be
with you — I don't wish to disparage my dear friends and acquaintances
here, there are so many of them and all so good, many so educated,
traveled, &c. some so handsome and witty, some rich &c. some among
the literary class — many young men — all good — many of them edu-
cated and polished and brilliant in conversation, &c — and I thought I
valued their society and friendship — and I do, for it is worth valuing —
But Douglass I will tell you the truth. You are so much closer to me than
any of them that there is no comparison — there has never passed so
much between them and me as we have — besides there is something
that takes down all artificial accomplishments, and that is a manly and
loving soul — My dearest comrade, I am sitting here writing to you very
late at night — I have been reading — it is indeed after 12, and my
mother and all the rest have gone to bed two hours ago, and I am here
above writing to you, and I enjoy it too. Although it is not much yet I
know it will please you dear boy. If you get this you must write and tell
me where and how you are. I hope you are quite well and with your dear
wife, for I know you have long wished to be with her, and I wish you to
give her my best respects and love too.

Douglass I haven't written any news for there is nothing particular I
have to write. Well, it is now past midnight, pretty well on to one o'clock,
and my sheet is mostly written out — so my dear darling boy, I must bid
you good night, or rather good morning, and I hope it may be God's will
we shall yet be with each other — but I must indeed bid you good night
my dear loving comrade, and the blessing of God on you by night and
day my darling boy.

Mrs. Louisa Whitman, Brooklyn

Washington, April 26, 1864.

Dearest Mother — Burnside's army passed through here yesterday. I saw George and walked with him in the regiment for some distance and had quite a talk. He is very well; he is very much tanned and looks hardy. I told him all the latest news from home. George stands it very well, and looks and behaves the same noble and good fellow he always was and always will be. It was on 14th st. I watched three hours before the 51st came along. I joined him just before they came to where the President and Gen. Burnside were standing with others on a balcony, and the interest of seeing me, etc., made George forget to notice the President and salute him. He was a little annoyed at forgetting it. I called his attention to it, but we had passed a little too far on, and George wouldn't turn round even ever so little. However, there was a great many more than half the army passed without noticing Mr. Lincoln and the others, for there was a great crowd all through the streets, especially here, and the place where the President stood was not conspicuous from the rest. The 9th Corps made a very fine show indeed. There were, I should think, five very full regiments of new black troops, under Gen. Ferrero. They looked and marched very well. It looked funny to see the President standing with his hat off to them just the same as the rest as they passed by. Then there [were the] Michigan regiments; one of them was a regiment of sharpshooters, partly composed of Indians. Then there was a pretty strong force of artillery and a middling force of cavalry — many New York, Pennsylvania, Massachusetts, R. I., etc., reg'ts. All except the blacks were veterans [that had] seen plenty of fighting. Mother, it is very different to see a real army of fighting men, from one of those shows in Brooklyn, or New York, or on Fort Greene. Mother, it was a curious sight to see these ranks after rank of our own dearest blood of men, mostly young, march by, worn and sunburnt and sweaty, with well-worn clothes and thin bundles, and knapsacks, tin cups, and some with frying pans strapt over their backs, all dirty and sweaty, nothing real neat about them except their muskets; but they were all as clean and bright as silver. They were four or five hours passing along, marching with wide ranks pretty quickly, too. It is a great sight to see an army 25 or 30,000 on the march. They are all so gay, too. Poor fellows, nothing dampens their spirits. They all got soaked with rain the night before. I saw Fred McReady and Capt. Sims, and Col. Le Gendre, etc. I don't know exactly where Burnside's army is going. Among other rumors it is said they [are] to go [with] the Army of the Potomac to act as a reserve force, etc. Another is

that they are to make a flank march, to go round and get Lee on the s■
etc. I have n't been out this morning and don't know what news — w■
know nothing, only that there is without doubt to be a terrible campaign
here in Virginia this summer, and that all who know deepest about it are
very serious about it. Mother, it is serious times. I do not feel to fret or
whimper, but in my heart and soul about our country, the forthcoming
campaign with all its vicissitudes and the wounded and slain — I dare
say, mother, I feel the reality more than some because I am in the midst
of its saddest results so much. Others may say what they like, I believe in
Grant and in Lincoln, too. I think Grant deserves to be trusted. He is
working continually. No one knows his plans; we will only know them
when he puts them in operation. Our army is very large here in Virginia
this spring, and they are still pouring in from east and west. You don't see
about it in the papers, but we have a very large army here.

Mother, I am first rate in health, thank God; I never was better. Dear
mother, have you got over all that distress and sickness in your head? You
must write particular about it. Dear brother Jeff, how are you, and how is
Matty, and how the dear little girls? Jeff, I believe the devil is in it about
my writing you; I have laid out so many weeks to write you a good long
letter, and something has shoved it off each time. Never mind, mother's
letters keep you posted. You must write, and don't forget to tell me all
about Sis. Is she as good and interesting as she was six months ago?
Mother, have you heard anything from Han? Mother, I have just had my
breakfast. I had it in my room — some hard biscuit warmed on the stove,
and a bowl of strong tea with good milk and sugar. I have given a
Michigan soldier his breakfast with me. He relished it, too; he has just
gone. Mother, I have just heard again that Burnside's troops are to be a
reserve to protect Washington, so there may be something in it.

Walt.

It is very fine weather here yesterday and today. The hospitals are very
full; they are putting up hundreds of hospital tents.

Mrs. Louisa Whitman, Brooklyn

Washington, June 14, 1864.

Dearest Mother. I am not feeling very well these days — the doctors have
told me not to come inside the hospitals for the present. I send there by a
friend every day; I send things and aid to some cases I know, and hear
from there also, but I do not go myself at present. It is probable that the

...s affected my system, and I find it worse than I
.....pells of faintness and very bad feeling in my head,
............and besides sore throat. My boarding place, 502
............., is a miserable place, very bad air. But I shall feel better
......know — the doctors say it will pass over — they have long told me
I was going in too strong. Some days I think it has all gone and I feel well
again, but in a few hours I have a spell again. Mother, I have not heard
anything of the 51st. I sent George's letter to Han. I have written to
George since. I shall write again to him in a day or two. If Mary comes
home, tell her I sent her my love. If I don't feel better before the end of
this week or beginning of next, I may come home for a week or fortnight
for a change. The rumor is very strong here that Grant is over the James
river on south side — but it is not in the papers. We are having quite cool
weather here. Mother, I want to see you and Jeff so much. I have been
working a little at copying, but have stopt it lately.

Walt.

Mrs. Louisa Whitman, Brooklyn

Washington, June 17, 1864.

Dearest Mother. I got your letter this morning. This place and the
hospitals seem to have got the better of me. I do not feel so badly this
forenoon — but I have bad nights and bad days too. Some of the spells
are pretty bad — still I am up some and around every day. The doctors
have told me for a fortnight I must leave; that I need an entire change of
air, etc.

I think I shall come home for a short time, and pretty soon.[7] (I will try
it two or three days yet though, and if I find my illness goes over I will
stay here yet awhile. All I think about is to be here if any thing should
happen to George).

We don't hear anything more of the army than you do there in the
papers.

Walt.

Mother, if I should come I will write a day or so before.

---

7. *I . . . soon*] Whitman returned to Brooklyn on June 23, 1864, and remained there for
nearly six months.

Charles W. Eldridge[8]

Brooklyn, N. Y.,
October 8, 1864.

. . . I am perhaps not so unconscionably hearty as before my sickness. We are deprest in spirits here about my brother George — if not killed, he is a prisoner — he was in the engagement of Sept. 30 — on the extreme left —— [9]

My book is not yet being printed. I still wish to stereotype it myself. I could easily still put it in the hands of a proper publisher then and make better terms with him.

If you write to William I wish you to enclose him this letter — I wish him to receive again my faithful friendship — while health and sense remain I cannot forget what he has been to me. I love him dearly ——

. . . The political meetings in New York and Brooklyn immense. I go to them as to shows — fireworks, cannon, clusters of gas lights, countless torches, banners and mottoes. 15, 20, 50,000 people — Per contra I occasionally go riding off in the country, in quiet lanes, or a sail on the water, and many times to . . . Coney Island.

All the signs are that Grant is going to strike farther, perhaps risk all. One feels solemn when one sees what depends. The military success though first class of war, is the least that depends.

Good by, dearest comrade. . . .

Walt.

---

8. *Charles W. Eldridge*] Whitman's publisher.

9. *George . . . left*] George Whitman was captured and taken prisoner at Danville, Virginia. He was released in a prisoner exchange several months later.

William D. O'Connor[10] [Washington, D. C.]

Brooklyn, January 6, 1865.

Dear friend

Your welcome letter of December 30 came safe. I have written & sent my application to Mr. Otto, & also a few lines to Mr. Ashton, with a copy of it. I am most desirous to get the appointment, as enclosing with the rest of the points, my attentions to the soldiers & to my poems, as you intimate.

— It may be *Drum-Taps* may come out this winter yet, (in the way I have mentioned in times past). It is in a state to put right through, a perfect copy being ready for the printers. I feel at last, & for the first time without any demur, that I am satisfied with it — content to have it go to the world verbatim & punctuatim. It is in my opinion superior to *Leaves of Grass* — certainly more perfect as a work of art, being adjusted in all its proportions, & its passion having the indispensable merit that though to the ordinary reader let loose with wildest abandon, the true artist can see it is yet under control. But I am perhaps mainly satisfied with *Drum-Taps* because it delivers my ambition of the task that has haunted me, namely, to express in a poem (& in the way I like, which is not at all by directly stating it) the pending action of this *Time & Land we swim in*, with all their large conflicting fluctuations of despair & hope, the shiftings, masses, & the whirl & deafening din, (yet over all, as by invisible hand, a definite purport & idea) — with the unprecedented anguish of wounded & suffering, the beautiful young men, in wholesale death & agony, everything sometimes as if blood color, & dripping blood. The book is therefore unprecedently sad, (as these days are, are they not?) — but it also has the blast of the trumpet, & the drum pounds & whirrs in it, & then an undertone of sweetest comradeship & human love, threading its steady thread inside the chaos, & heard at every lull & interstice thereof — truly, also it has clear notes of faith & triumph.

—— *Drum-Taps* has none of the perturbations of *Leaves of Grass*. I am satisfied with *Leaves of Grass*, (by far the most of it) as expressing what was intended, namely, to express by sharp-cut self assertion, One's Self & also, or may be still more, to map out, to throw together for American use, a gigantic embryo or skeleton of Personality, — fit for the

---

10. *William D. O'Connor*] A friend of Eldridge's, O'Connor met Whitman in the publisher's office and the two became good friends. When Whitman was dismissed from his post in the Indian Bureau in June 1865, for writing an "indecent book" (*Leaves of Grass*), O'Connor defended him by writing his famous pamphlet, *The Good Gray Poet*.

West, for native models — but there are a few things I shall carefully eliminate in the next issue, & a few more I shall considerably change.

I see I have said I consider *Drum-Taps* superior to *Leaves of Grass*. I probably mean as a piece of art, & from the more simple & winning nature of the subject, & also because I have in it only succeeded to my satisfaction in removing all superfluity from it, verbal superfluity I mean, I delight to make a poem where I feel clear that not a word but is indispensable part thereof & of my meaning.

Still *Leaves of Grass* is dear to me, always dearest to me, as my first born, as daughter of my life's first hopes, doubts, & the putting in form of those days' efforts & aspirations — true, I see now, with some things in it I should not put in if I were to write now, but yet I shall certainly let them stand, even if but for proofs of phases passed away.

Mother and all home are well as usual. Not a word for over three months from my brother George — the probabilities are most gloomy. — I see the Howells now & then. I am well, but need to leave here — need a change. If you see Miss Howard tell her Jesse Mullery has been to see me — came yesterday & has just left this forenoon. He talked of nothing but her. His life is saved, & he will have tolerably good strength & health, at least for present. His address is ward 7 Centre St Hospital Newark New Jersey. I was up at Mrs. Price's the other night. She is better this winter. Mrs. Paulina Wright Davis is stopping with her this winter. I have sent a paper with sketch of Hospital Visits, to Dr. Wm. F. Channing. I cannot forgive myself for not acknowledging his assistance for the Hospitals, by letter at the time. I send you another paper also, as you might like it. I take it by a line in your letter that Charles Eldridge has not gone to Boston. I have been reading the strange articles from the Richmond press. A thousand Satans baffled with terror, hatred, malignant squirming, appear in every paragraph. Little California is playing around me as I finish, & has been for half an hour. Love to dear Nelly & Jeannie & all.

Walt Whitman

Mrs. Irwin, ——, Pennsylvania[11]

[May, 1865]

Dear madam: No doubt you and Frank's friends have heard the sad fact of his death in hospital here, through his uncle, or the lady from Baltimore, who took his things. (I have not seen them, only heard of them visiting Frank.) I will write you a few lines — as a casual friend that sat by his death-bed. Your son, corporal Frank H. Irwin, was wounded near Fort Fisher, Virginia, March 25th, 1865 — the wound was in the left knee, pretty bad. He was sent up to Washington, was receiv'd in Ward C, Armory-square hospital, March 28th — the wound became worse, and on the 4th of April the leg was amputated a little above the knee — the operation was perform'd by Dr. Bliss, one of the best surgeons in the army — he did the whole operation himself — there was a good deal of bad matter gather'd — the bullet was found in the knee. For a couple of weeks afterwards he was doing pretty well. I visited and sat by him frequently, as he was fond of having me. The last ten or twelve days of April I saw that his case was critical. He previously had some fever, with cold spells. The last week in April he was much of the time flighty — but always mild and gentle. He died first of May. The actual cause of death was pyaemia, (the absorption of the matter in the system instead of its discharge.) Frank, as far as I saw, had everything requisite in surgical treatment, nursing, &c. He had watches much of the time. He was so good and well-behaved and affectionate, I myself liked him very much. I was in the habit of coming in afternoons and sitting by him, and soothing him, and he liked to have me — liked to put his arm out and lay his hand on my knee — would keep it so a long while. Toward the last he was more restless and flighty at night — often fancied himself with his regiment — by his talk sometimes seem'd as if his feelings were hurt by being blamed by his officers for something he was entirely innocent of — said, "I never in my life was thought capable of such a thing, and never was." At other times he would fancy himself talking as it seem'd to children or such like, his relatives I suppose, and giving them good advice; would talk to them a long while. All the time he was out of his head not one single bad word or idea escaped him. It was remark'd that many a man's conversation in his senses was not half as good as Frank's

---

11. *Mrs. Irwin . . . Pennsylvania*] This letter appears in *Memoranda during the War* and in *Specimen Days in America* under the heading "Death of a Pennsylvania Soldier."

delirium. He seem'd quite willing to die — he had become very weak and had suffer'd a good deal, and was perfectly resign'd, poor boy. I do not know his past life, but I feel as if it must have been good. At any rate what I saw of him here, under the most trying circumstances, with a painful wound, and among strangers, I can say that he behaved so brave, so composed, and so sweet and affectionate, it could not be surpass'd. And now like many other noble and good men, after serving his country as a soldier, he has yielded up his young life at the very outset in her service. Such things are gloomy — yet there is a text, "God doeth all things well" — the meaning of which, after due time, appears to the soul.

I thought perhaps a few words, though from a stranger, about your son, from one who was with him at the last, might be worth while — for I loved the young man, though I but saw him immediately to lose him. I am merely a friend visiting the hospitals occasionally to cheer the wounded and sick.

W. W.

Mrs. Louisa Whitman, Brooklyn

Washington, Thursday, May 25, '65

Dear Mother, I received your letter of the 22d — I feel uneasy about you all the time, & hope I shall get a letter to-day, & find you have recovered.

Well, the Review is over, & it was very grand — it was too much & too impressive, to be described — but you will see a good deal about it in the papers. If you can imagine a great wide avenue like Flatbush avenue, quite flat, & stretching as far as you can see with a great white building half as big as Fort Greene on a hill at the commencement of the avenue, and then through this avenue marching solid ranks of soldiers, 20 or 25 abreast, just marching steady all day long for two days without intermission, one regiment after another, real war-worn soldiers, that have been marching & fighting for years — sometimes for an hour nothing but cavalry, just solid ranks, on good horses, with sabres glistening & carbines hanging by their saddles, & their clothes showing hard service, but they mostly all good-looking hardy young men — then great masses of guns, batteries of cannon, four or six abreast, each drawn by six horses, with the gunners seated on the ammunition wagons — & these perhaps a long while in passing, nothing but batteries, — (it seemed as if all the cannon in the world were here) — then great battalions of blacks, with axes & shovels & pick axes, (real Southern darkies, black as tar) — then again hour after hour the old infantry regiments, the men all sunburnt — nearly every one with some old tatter all in shreds, (that *had been* a costly and beautiful *flag*) — the great drum corps of sixty or eighty drummers massed at the heads of the brigades, playing away — now & then a fine brass band, — but oftener nothing but the drums & whistling fifes, — but they sounded very lively — (perhaps a band of sixty drums & fifteen or twenty fifes playing "Lannigan's ball") — the different corps banners, the generals with their staffs &c — the Western Army, led by Gen. Sherman, (old Bill, the soldiers all call him) — well, dear mother, that is a brief sketch, give you some idea of the great panorama of the Armies that have been passing through here the last two days.

— I saw the President several times, stood close by him, & took a good look at him — & like his expression much — he is very plain & substantial — it seemed wonderful that just that plain middling-sized ordinary man, dressed in black, without the least badge or ornament, should be the master of all these myriads of soldiers, the best that ever trod the earth, with forty or fifty Major-Generals, around him or riding by with their broad yellow-satin belts around their waists, — and of all the artillery & cavalry, — to say nothing of all the Forts & ships, &c. &c. — I saw Gen. Grant too several times — He is the noblest Roman of them all — none of the pictures do justice to him — about sundown I saw him again riding on a large fine horse, with his hat off in answer to the hurrahs — he rode by where I stood, & I saw him well, as he rode by on a slow canter, with nothing but a single orderly after him — He looks like a good man — (& I believe there is much in looks) — I saw Gen. Meade, Gen. Thomas, Secretary Stanton, & lots of other celebrated government officers & generals — but the *rank* and *file* was the greatest sight of all.

The 51st was in the line Tuesday with the 9th Corps. I saw George but did not get a chance to speak to him. He is well. George is now *Major* George W. Whitman, — has been commissioned & mustered in. (Col. Wright & Col. Shephard have done it, I think.) The 51st is over to the Old Convalescent camp, between here and Alexandria, doing provost duty. It, the old camp is now called Amgur General Hospital. If you should write direct,

Major G. W. Whitman
51st New York V. V.
on provost duty at
Amgur Gen'l Hospital
near Alexandria Va

It is thought that the 51st will not be mustered out for the present — It is thought the Government will retain the reenlisted veteran regiments, such as the 51st—If that is so George will remain as he is for the summer, or most of it—The reason I haven't seen him is, I knew they had left provost duty in the Prince st. prison, but didn't know where they had gone till Tuesday—I saw Capt. Caldwell Tuesday, also Col. Wright Tuesday night—they said they all have pleasant quarters over there.

Dear brother Jeff, I was very sorry you wasnt able to come on to see the Review—we had perfect weather & everything just as it should be—the streets now are full of soldiers scattered around loose, as the armies are in camp near here getting ready to be mustered out.—I am quite well & visit the Hospitals the same.—Mother you didn't write whether you got the package of 5 *Drum-Taps*—I keep thinking about you every few minutes all day—I wish I was home a couple of days—Jeff, you will take this acc't of the Review, same as if it were written to you.

Walt.

Alphabetical List of Poem Titles

Alphabetical List of Poem First Lines